SOLUTIONS

D0047439

MARIE CURIE
and the Discovery of Radium

BY ANN E. STEINKE

Illustrated by Roger Xavier

BARRON'S

This book is dedicated to the memory of my father,
who lives on in my heart; and to my mother, who
continues on.

Note: In this book the feminine version of the Polish name Sklodowski is spelled with
an *a*, instead of an *i*. This is the custom in that country.

First edition published 1987
by Barron's Educational Series, Inc.

All inquiries should be addressed to:
Barron's Educational Series, Inc.
250 Wireless Blvd.
Hauppauge, NY 11788

Library of Congress Catalog Card No. 87-24392

International Standard Book No. 0-8120-3924-6

Library of Congress Cataloging-in-Publication Data

Steinke, Anne.
    Marie Curie and the discovery of radium / by Anne Steinke.
    — 1st ed.
    p. cm.
    Includes index.
    Summary: Examines the life of the scientist Marie Curie, her
background and her discovery of radium.
    ISBN 0-8120-3924-6
    1. Curie, Marie, 1867-1934 — Juvenile literature. 2. Radium —
Juvenile literature. 2. Chemists — Poland — Biography — Juvenile
literature. [1. Curie, Marie, 1867-1934. 2. Chemists.]
I. Title
QD22.C8S78   1987
540.92'4 — dc19
[B]   87-24392
[92]   CIP
                                                       AC

Printed in the United States of America
23   9693   9876543

CONTENTS

CHAPTER ONE

Small Beginnings

In 1867, it was not unusual for mothers to give birth to their babies at home. It was unusual, however, for them to give birth at a school. But this is exactly what Marie Curie's mother did. On November 7, 1867, Marya Salomee Sklodowska was born in the Freta Street Boarding School for girls in Warsaw, Poland. The world later would know Marya Sklodowska as Marie Curie.

Mrs. Sklodowska was the principal of the Freta school. She was a beautiful woman, with soft gray eyes and strong features. She wore her dark hair in smooth braids pinned up over her ears. Marya's father taught physics at another school in Warsaw.

The Sklodowski family lived together in a small apartment right in the Freta school. The apartment was given to them as part of Mrs. Sklodowska's salary. When Marie was born, Mrs. Sklodowska had been working at the school for almost eight years. Little Marya was her fifth, and last, child.

The Sklodowski children were all called by nicknames, and Marya had several. Sometimes her mother called her "My Anciupecio." But usually she was called Manyusya, or Manya for short. Sofia, the oldest girl, was

1

called Zosia. Joseph, the second oldest, was the only boy. He was nicknamed Jozio. Bronislawa was known as Bronya, and Helena was shortened to Hela.

Mr. Sklodowski knew he would need more money to support his growing family. He took a new job at a high school for boys, on Novolipki Street. The family was given another apartment right in the school as part of his salary. Mr. Sklodowski's new position was vice-principal of the school, as well as professor of mathematics and physics.

At this time, Poland was ruled over by Russia, Austria, and Germany. In 1863, the Polish people had revolted. But the Germans and Russians had thousands of well-trained troops, and the Poles were crushed. The Sklodowski family loved Poland, and, like all Poles, they wanted it to be free again.

In many schools, teaching Polish history was strictly forbidden. Students learned only Russian history, and they had to read and speak only Russian. Nevertheless, Manya's father and mother encouraged their children to do well in school. All the children loved school, but none of them found it as easy as Manya did. When she was four years old, the family learned just how smart she was.

The Sklodowskis were vacationing with relatives in the Polish countryside. Seven-year-old Bronya was supposed to spend some time studying her alphabet. She thought studying was so boring, that she decided to make it more fun by playing a game with little Manya. Bronya would be the teacher and Manya would be the student!

Marie with parents and older sister, Bronya.

The two girls spent many hours playing with cardboard cutouts of the alphabet.

Sometime later, Manya and her parents were listening to Bronya read from a book as part of her lessons. Poor Bronya was having a hard time and kept stumbling over the words. Impatiently, Manya took the book from Bronya's hands, and began reading the first sentence— without one mistake!

There was silence. Surely, Manya thought, that meant her parents were impressed. She went on to read the next sentence. But looking up, Manya did *not* see pleased faces. Her parents were stunned, and Bronya was pouting. Manya thought she had done something terrible!

"Beg pardon" Manya cried. "I didn't do it on purpose. It's not Bronya's fault. It's only because it was so easy!"

Her parents were disturbed that their little Manya was so advanced. They thought it might be harmful for one so young to be reading. For sometime after that, they did not allow her near a book. Manya would ask timidly, "I . . . may I read?" Her mother would say, "I wish you would go into the garden instead. It's so beautiful today!" Or Mrs. Sklodowska asked Manya to play with her dolls or blocks. Sometimes the answer was, "Sing a song, Manya."

Often, 11-year-old Zosia was asked to take Manya to the garden. With one last look at the books, out Manya went. She was always ready to go to the garden with Zosia. There, she could hear her older sister's wonderful stories. Manya loved to watch Zosia tell stories. She admired her sister's blonde hair and gray eyes. Zosia could entertain Manya for hours. Manya thought no one in the world could tell a tale like Zosia could. Sometimes, Zosia made up funny plays, and performed them for Manya and the other children. Little Manya didn't always understand the plays, but she loved them, anyway. Zosia's stories made up for the books Manya couldn't have.

At night, the family liked to gather in Mr. Sklodowski's study. The older children sat around the desk and did their school work, while Mr. Sklodowski read the newspaper or a book.

Mrs. Sklodowska sat in the corner making shoes for her growing family. She had taught herself the special skills she needed for this difficult work. Ever since the family had moved to the new apartment on Novolipki Street, she hadn't been able to work outside the home. Mrs. Sklodowska was ill with tuberculosis. At that time, there was little that doctors could do about the disease. As the children were small, they were not told about their mother's illness. The children knew their mother loved them, but she never showed it by either kissing or hugging them. The only caress she gave her little Manyusya was to run her hands over the tiny girl's short, unruly curls. She was afraid if she got too close to her children, they would catch her sickness. It was only when the children were much older that they understood this.

Now, to save money, Mrs. Sklodowska toiled over the leather and shoemaker's tools. It was tiring work, but she was not one to complain. She knew the family did not have enough money. If she had to make them shoes to help out, then that's what she would do. As a grown woman, Manya would have the same sense of duty as her mother did, and she would work hard to do what was needed.

Wearing the black high topped shoes her mother had made, little Manya walked about the study. She looked at all her favorite things there. First she stopped at the clock sitting on the desk. It was made out of a bright green mineral called malachite. Then, on to the round table brought back from Palermo, Italy, by a cousin. The top of the desk was made of squares of different kinds of marble, and it looked like a checkerboard. Next, Manya stared up at something her father called a barometer. Its white dial had long glittering pointers painted gold. The

Marie as a child viewing physics apparatus in her father's workroom.

barometer was strange and mysterious to Manya, but the most interesting thing in the whole study was her father's bookcase.

Manya peered through the glass doors of the tall bookcase for a long time. Its shelves were full of amazing things. She saw odd instruments and glass tubes and small scales. There were also specimens of minerals, which just looked like rocks to the little girl. There was even a gold leaf electroscope, an instrument used for detecting electricity.

A new rule at Mr. Sklodowski's school had cut down on the amount of time teachers could spend teaching science. Professor Sklodowski had kept his bookcase shut after that. He never took those wonderful items from the shelves again.

Manya thought the things in her father's bookcase were fascinating, even if she didn't know what they were. But someday Manya would know. Someday she would study physics, the subject her father taught. Physics is a science that tells *how* things work and *why* they work. A scientist needs certain instruments that enable him or her to learn how and why things work. It was his scientific instruments that Mr. Sklodowski kept in his bookcase. One day, Manya's father told her a name for all the instruments.

"Phy-sics app-a-ra-tus."

Little Manya was introduced to her first scientific term, and she remembered it all her life.

CHAPTER TWO

The Painful Years

In the fall of 1873, Manya was six years old. Ever since her mother had been unable to work, the family had trouble making ends meet. Now, Mr. Sklodowski was having difficulties at the high school on Novolipki Street, where he taught. The Principal, Mr. Ivanov, did not like Mr. Sklodowski. Mr. Ivanov didn't feel that the professor showed him the right amount of respect. Once, Mr. Sklodowski said something to Mr. Ivanov that made the principal especially angry. Mr. Ivanov had criticized one of Professor Sklodowski's students for not writing Russian properly. Professor Sklodowski replied that sometimes *Mr. Ivanov* didn't write Russian properly either! It was an accusation Mr. Ivanov never forgot. He'd been waiting for a chance to get even with this bold Polish teacher, and he succeeded that fall. He managed to have Mr. Sklodowski's title of vice principal taken away. The Sklodowskis were no longer allowed to live in the apartment in the school. Mr. Ivanov also had the professor's salary cut back. Now Mr. Sklodowski couldn't earn enough money, so the family had to move again.

After several moves, they finally settled into a large apartment in a building on the corner of Novolopki and

Carmelite streets. In order to bring in more money, Mr. Sklodowski also had some of his students move in with the family. The boys paid rent, and, in return, got their food, beds, and private lessons from Mr. Sklodowski.

It was a difficult arrangement for the family. The apartment was too small for everyone to have a bedroom. Manya had to sleep on a couch in the dining room. She had to be up and dressed by 6 o'clock every morning so everybody else in the house could sit down and eat breakfast.

At first, three or four boys lived with the family. Later, eight of them lived as boarders in the Sklodowski house. There was noise and activity everywhere. It was not a peaceful place in which to live or study.

Mr. Sklodowski needed the extra money because his wife was becoming sicker all the time. He wanted to send her to a healthier climate, where she might get better. He managed to save enough money to send her and Zosia to the Riviera in Nice, France, for a year. But when she came back Mrs. Sklodowska looked even worse. She had grown thin and weak. She coughed up blood, which she tried to hide in her handkerchief. The year in France hadn't done her any good.

The following year even more distress came the family's way. One of the students living with them had typhus, a terribly contagious disease. Bronya and Zosia caught typhus and were sick for weeks. In one room, Mrs. Sklodowska was coughing. In another room, the two sisters were burning up with an awful fever. The sickness was too much for Zosia. In January of 1876, the

Manya at Miss Sikorska's boarding school for girls.

beautiful, blonde girl lost her battle. The family followed Zosia's funeral down Carmelite street. Bronya, who was still sick in bed, cried into her pillow. Zosia's weeping mother was also unable to leave the apartment. She dragged herself from window to window, following the coffin with her eyes until she could no longer see it.

When she was 10 years old, Manya, along with Hela, began attending Miss Sikorska's boarding school for girls. Although they didn't live in the school, they wore the same school uniform as the rest of the girls. It was a navy blue wool dress, with steel buttons and a stiff, starched white collar. Manya and Hela were in the same class, even though Manya was two years younger than the rest of the girls.

Their teacher was Antonina Tupalska. Her face was heavy and plain, and her clothing was never in style. Her students gave her the affectionate nickname of "Tupsia." She was very fond of little Manya. In spite of being younger than the rest of the girls, Manya was one of her brightest pupils.

Miss Sikorska's school was doing something the Russian government had forbidden. The teachers were secretly teaching Polish history! If the Russians found out, the school would be in terrible trouble.

A system had been worked out to keep the school from being caught teaching the forbidden Polish. Mr. Hornberg, the Russian inspector of private boarding schools in Warsaw, sometimes made surprise visits. When he arrived at the front door of the school, the janitor would push a button that rang a bell on the landing of the stairway.

When the bell sounded, two long rings followed by two short rings, everyone had her own job to do. Four girls filled their aprons with the books on Polish history. Then they ran to hide them in the rooms where the girls who lived at the school slept. Breathless, they ran back to their seats, then pulled out their sewing projects.

When Mr. Hornberg entered the room, the entire class would be busy sewing and trying to look innocent. Tuspia, herself a little out of breath, would try to appear calm. Then would come the part that Manya, shy and frightened, hated most.

"Please call on one of these young people," Mr. Hornberg would tell Tupsia. Everyone knew what was going to happen next. Mr. Hornberg would question the unfortunate student about Russia, its past and present.

Little Manya, sitting in her seat in the third row, prayed that Tupsia wouldn't choose her. But Tupsia knew that of all the students Manya was the smartest and knew the most. The youngest student was usually the one who had to stand and answer the hateful questions.

Sometimes Mr. Hornberg would make her recite the Lord's Prayer in Russian. Sometimes she had to name the five czars who had ruled Russia since Catherine II.

Then would always come the most hated question of all: "Who rules over us?"

Even at age 10, Manya loved Poland and wanted it to be free. Now, she would have to admit that the Poles were not free, that "His Majesty Alexander II, Czar of All the Russias" was the one who ruled them!

Finally, when he was satisfied with Manya's answers, Mr. Hornberg would leave. Afterwards, Manya would always burst into tears.

"Come here, my little soul," Tuspia would say and kiss her star pupil on the forehead.

After school Manya and Hela's Aunt Lucia would come to walk her nieces home. Sometimes the girls would visit the church Mrs. Sklodowska had attended before she became too sick to leave the apartment. When she was well, Mrs. Sklodowska, who was Catholic, went almost every day to the church named the Chapel of Our Lady. She had loved the old church with it's arched doors,

Manya was the smartest and knew the most.

its square tower, and steps made of red stone worn away from centuries of use. Surely God would reward someone so faithful, Manya hoped. There, in the church her mother had loved, little Manya prayed on her knees. Please, would Jesus not take her beloved Mother? It was enough that Zosia was gone. Manya would rather that she die in her mother's place, than lose her, too!

13

Afterwards the girls and their aunt would leave the church, which overlooked the Vistula River, and head home.

In the evening, Manya, Hela, Jozio, and Bronya gathered in the dining room and studied at the table. Manya, however, didn't have to study long. Her mind was so quick, she could read a poem only two times and recite it from memory without one mistake.

Manya could concentrate on her studies so well, she wasn't aware of anything going on around her. After studying, she pulled out a book she was reading for pleasure, and devoted herself to it with the same attention. Her power of concentration furnished her brother, sisters, and cousin Henrietta with plenty of amusement. Many times, as a joke, they would take chairs and build them into a scaffold all around Manya. Then, when she had finished reading, she'd stand up and knock all the chairs down with a great crash. While everyone else thought this was great fun, Manya was not amused.

"That's stupid!" would be her reaction, and off she'd go to read somewhere else.

Manya retreated into her books because they took her away from a world that often frightened her. If she was reading, she didn't have to think about the Russians or visits from Mr. Hornberg. She didn't have to look at the sad, overworked face of her father, or hear her mother coughing. She didn't have to think about dragging herself from bed at six o'clock the next morning. To escape from these harsh things in her life, she read hungrily, and she read everything—poetry, adventure stories, even technical books that belonged to her father.

But all the books in the world couldn't save Manya from what she feared most. On May 9, 1878, her mother gathered her beloved family around her bedside and told them good-bye. Her last words were, "I love you."

The family mourned her death for several years. Black curtains were hung on the windows of the apartment. Into storage went the girls' pretty dresses of different colors. They were replaced by garments of black. Joseph and his father wore suits of somber black also. Even the notepaper they used had black edges. The Sklodowski house was a brooding, sorrowful place for a young girl to grow up in. The long mourning dragged out the agony Manya felt over her mother's death. She could not help but notice how the prolonged period of grief made her father age faster than he should have. After her mother's death, Manya felt lost and abandoned. She buried herself, even more, in her books and studies.

CHAPTER THREE

Growing Up

B y the time Manya entered high school, the family had moved from the apartment on Carmelite Street to one on Leschen Street. It was a much larger apartment, situated on the first floor. At last Manya didn't have to sleep in the dining room so the boarders could have the bedrooms.

Bronya and Joseph had graduated from high school at the top of their classes. Each had won gold medals in recognition of their academic excellence. Hela and Manya attended a Russian high school on Krakonsky Boulevard. Russian high schools were the only ones that gave out officially recognized diplomas.

In those days, women were not allowed to get a higher education at a college or university. Bronya was forced to stay home after she graduated and run the house since she was unable to continue her studies. All the Sklodowski girls wished they could attend the University of Warsaw, but only Joseph was able to advance his schooling. He was attending the Faculty of Medicine and was the envy of his sisters.

Every morning Hela and Manya would pack their lunches of bread, apples, and Polish sausages in a cloth bag and leave for school. On her way there, Manya would

Manya & Bronya.

stop for her friend Kazia Przyborovska. Kazia and Manya always made fun of their Russian teachers and administrators.

Kazia and Manya liked their Polish teachers, however. They especially liked Mr. Glass, the handsome young teacher of mathematics. They also liked Mr. Slosarski, the professor of natural sciences. Both girls were good students, too, especially Manya who loved school better than anything else. She wrote to Kazia once during a vacation and said "I like school. . . . I must tell you that I love it."

On June 12, 1883, Manya graduated from high school, the third member of her family to win a gold medal. She had studied hard and done very well. Her father thought that she ought to have a reward *and* a rest. The doctors agreed. They diagnosed her as having a nervous breakdown, and said it was the strain of years of hard studying. Manya was sent to visit relatives in the country for almost a whole year.

During those months of vacation she had a wonderful time. She went on sleigh rides and picnics and she went to her first "kulig." A kulig was a very special occasion. It was like a ball, but much grander—and lasted much longer! It started one evening in winter, while the land lay under its blanket of snow. Manya and her cousins rode in two sleighs, with handsome young men in peasant costumes accompanying them on horseback. Manya and her cousins were also in costume. Manya's was a velvet jacket worn over a white embroidered dress with puffed sleeves. Long ribbons of many colors fell from a "crown" of wheat on her head. The guests would begin the dance at one place, a barn or someone's house. Then, by sleigh, they would go to the next place. They moved from house to house all night and into the next morning. Sometimes the dance went on through the second night!

This was a happy time for Manya. She wrote about her first kulig to her friend Kazia.

"I have been to a *kulig*. You can't imagine how delightful it is, especially when the clothes are beautiful. . . . At eight o'clock in the morning we danced the last dance."

She also wrote to Kazia that for the first time she had no schedule. "I get up sometimes at ten o'clock, sometimes at four or five (morning, not evening!). I read no serious books." Manya had spent years and years reading books well beyond her level. She felt "incredibly stupid," but she was enjoying the rest.

Manya's love for Poland was made even greater by her vacation in the countryside. She especially loved the Carpathian mountains, which rim Poland on its southern border. For Manya, their glittering summits, covered in snow, were awesome. High up in the peaks was a little lake called "The Eye of the Sea." She spent hours by its pure, icy waters. It enchanted her. That year Manya spent in the country and in the mountains gave her a sense of wonder and love of Poland that would stay with her all her life.

At the end of the year, Manya returned to Warsaw. Her father had moved back to another apartment on Novolopki Street.

Now that Manya was almost seventeen, she had to decide what she wanted to do with her life. She had been an excellent all-around student. She knew she wanted to help the children of Poland and felt the only way she could was to be a teacher.

Mr. Sklodowski was getting older. He was plumper now. His neat beard was turning grey, and his hairline was receding. It had become hard for him to care for the boys who stayed with him. He decided not to take in boarders anymore. That meant there was less money to support his family. To help him out Manya, Bronya, Joseph, and Hela all had to go out and earn a living.

There were very few jobs available for young people in Poland at this time. Most of them became tutors, so this was what the four children set out to do. The girls put ads in the papers that read, "Lessons in arithmetic, geometry, French, by young lady with diploma." Joseph's ad read, "Medical student will do private tutoring." After her year of having fun, Manya now had to walk through the streets of Warsaw from one tutoring job to another. She gave the private lessons for a few Polish dollars, called rubles, a month.

It was during this time that Manya and Bronya joined a group called the "Floating University." This group tried to provide extra education for young people who had graduated from high school, but couldn't attend the university. The Russians were against the Polish people becoming educated, so the Floating University was started. They met in secret and in different places all the time so that the Russians wouldn't catch them. Some of the "instructors" were actually school teachers, but others were simply students sharing what they knew. Eight or 10 people would meet in someone's home, listen to lectures, and pass pamphlets or articles to each other. Manya listened to lessons on anatomy, natural history, and sociology. In turn she gave lessons to women from poor families.

At this time, people were very interested in chemistry and biology. This was because many important scientific discoveries were being made. Charles Darwin had published his theory on how humans evolved from lower animals. Louis Pasteur had recently discovered vaccinations for diseases like rabies. These discoveries, along with others, gave science new importance. People thought science could someday solve all their problems. When Manya entered the Floating University, its emphasis on science naturally influenced her.

For a while, simply being members of the Floating University satisfied the desire for knowledge that Bronya and Manya felt. But eventually, it wasn't enough. Bronya wanted very badly to go to Paris, France, and attend a university there. Her dream was to get a doctor's degree, then come home to Poland and help her people.

Time and time again, she would sit down with paper and ink and figure out how much money she had and how much more she needed before she could see her dream come true. Month after month went by, and still her tutoring pay wasn't enough.

So one day, Manya came to Bronya with a plan. Bronya should go to Paris right away and spend what money she had already saved. Then Manya and Mr. Sklo-dowski would send her the money she needed to complete the five years of schooling necessary to be a doctor.

Bronya objected. "You don't hope to make enough money to support yourself *and* me, and still be able to save, do you?" she asked.

Manya knew it wouldn't be possible to make enough tutoring. She told Bronya her plan. "I am going to get a job as a governess in a family," she said. "With board, lodgings, and laundry all free, I shall save four hundred rubles a year in wages, perhaps more."

Bronya's eyes filled with tears. People would look down on Manya. Then, governesses were considered little better than servants. Bronya knew what a sacrifice her little sister was willing to make so that she could go to Paris. Bronya couldn't stand the thought. "Why should I be the first to go?" she argued. "Why not the other way around? You are so gifted, probably more gifted than I am. You would succeed very quickly. Why should *I* go?"

Manya argued that Bronya was 20 and she was 17. The elder should go first. Manya had lots of time to wait. She said, "When you have your practice you can bury me in gold." When Manya was ready to go to the university, it would be Bronya's turn to help her. Meanwhile, she would work as a governess and save some of her pay for herself, too.

Finally, Bronya could object no more. In the fall of 1885, she went off to Paris, and Manya set out to find work for herself as a governess.

CHAPTER FOUR

The Sacrifice

With the help of an employment agency, Manya found her first job as a governess for a family in Warsaw. She was not happy with the family. In a letter to her cousin, Henrietta, Manya complained, "My relations with Mrs. B. had become so icy that I could not endure it any longer and told her so. It was one of those rich houses where they speak French when there is company, but they don't pay their bills for six months."

Manya also realized that she couldn't make enough money in Warsaw. She had wanted to remain there so she could still go to the Floating University and be near her family. But governesses in the country were paid more than governesses in the city. She had to find a position out in the country so she could make enough money to send some to Bronya and save for her own education.

So, in January, 1886, she headed for her new job with the Zorawski family. They lived 100 kilometers, or about sixty-two miles, from Warsaw. It took her three hours by train, then four hours by sleigh, to get to their home. She hated leaving her father, but she was being paid five hundred rubles a year. With such a salary, she could send

Marie tutoring neighborhood children.

Bronya 15 to 20 rubles a month. Manya was very generous. That many rubles was almost half her pay!

This family was nicer to her than the one in Warsaw had been. They were well off, but not extremely rich. Their house was an old fashioned two-storied one, with a shingled roof sloping down to stuccoed walls. There was a large garden surrounded by ash trees, and even a croquet ground on the lawn. Manya soon became friends with their oldest daughter, 18-year-old Bronka. Her job was to teach both Bronka, and 10-year-old Andzia. She spent seven hours a day teaching.

One day she met some of the peasant children who lived in a nearby village. She decided to try to teach them about Polish history and its language. If any of them had been able to go to school at all, they had learned only Russian. Manya's dream was to help the children of Poland learn to read and write the language of their homeland. Now she could start to do that in a small way. Mr. Zorawski gave her permission as long as she did it on her own time and in her own room. She spent as much as five hours a day trying to teach the ignorant village children. Some of these "children" were almost 18 years old! It took a long time, but some of them finally learned to read and write Polish. Manya wished their parents could learn also.

Manya was in the country, but instead of beautiful landscapes with trees and mountains, the house was surrounded by acres and acres of beet fields. Nearby was a huge, smoke-belching factory, where the beets were turned into sugar. Surprisingly, the factory offered Manya a way to spend the hours when she wasn't working. It had a library from which she could borrow books. During the next few years, she taught and read, taught and read. Gradually she discovered she had a preference for mathematics and physics.

Manya felt her scientific education was not very good. She had a dream that someday she would get the kind of education she wanted. But she knew she would have to leave Poland to get it. She would have to go to France, to the famous university in Paris called the Sorbonne. Manya hoped to keep learning so that when she finally got to the Sorbonne she would know as much as everyone else. She felt she could accomplish this by reading as much as possible in the factory library.

The Zorawski family had three sons who were away in Warsaw. Two were at boarding schools, and the oldest one was attending the university there. His name was Casimir. When he came home on vacation, he was very impressed with the new governess. She was a good dancer; she was witty and enjoyed sports like rowing, skating, and riding horses. She was so different from the girls he knew, who talked about silly subjects and would never do anything athletic. He fell madly in love with Manya. He was handsome and charming, and she fell in love with him, too. It was natural that they wanted to get married, so he went to his parents to get permission. Neither Casimir nor Manya expected any objections. After all, Casimir's parents treated Manya almost as if she was one of their children. Hadn't they been kind to her? Why, they even gave Manya presents on her birthday, and had invited her father and brother and sister to their home. So imagine the young couple's shock when the parents reacted so violently to Casimir's request. His father became very angry, and his mother almost fainted!

He, a young man from a rich family, wanted to marry a poor working girl? Never! He had to be crazy. Absolutely not, they said, and Casimir was too weak to fight them. He went back to school and left Manya broken-hearted.

For Manya there was no choice but to stay with the family and keep on earning money. Bronya, away in

Paris, still needed her help. Besides, she had to save for her own education which she still hoped to get. She couldn't run away. Duty called her. But she decided she would never fall in love again. Instead, she'd devote her energies to her dream of educating herself. Now she spent even more time reading her library books, filling her head with science. Some nights she would stay up as late as two o'clock in the morning reading.

In April, 1888, things began looking up for her father in Warsaw. He accepted a position as director of a reform school located just outside of Warsaw. The job paid well, and it allowed Mr. Sklodowski to send money to Bronya. Bronya wrote Manya and told her she did not need to send her any more money. Manya was free to save her hard earned pay for herself. Bronya also told her father to save eight rubles out of the 40 he wanted to send her every month. The eight rubles were to repay Manya. Bronya's loving little sister had been sending money faithfully for over two years.

Even though Manya could keep all her pay for herself now, she was not free to leave the Zorawskis. She had agreed to work for them for three years and she still had a year to go. Manya intended to keep her side of the agreement. So for one more year, she taught the Zorawski children.

She spent that year studying as well. But she was not satisfied with just her books. Manya wanted to be able to do more than simply read about science. She wanted to work in a laboratory, to do actual experiments.

She wrote of her desires to her brother Joseph. "I

am learning chemistry from a book. You can imagine how little I get out of that. But what can I do, as I have no place to make experiments or do practical work?"

Manya was beginning to think and feel like a scientist.

Manya was often depressed by her life during these days. Sometimes she would fall into a what she called a "black melancholy" because of the dreary countryside and the endless cold and wind. But she didn't have much time to feel sorry for herself. Her life was filled with work.

In November of 1888, Manya turned 21 years old. She had been working for the Zorawski family for almost two years. When she had left high school, she had been a slightly pudgy adolescent. Now she was a slim, pretty, young woman. She wrote a letter to her cousin Henrietta and told Henrietta how people thought she had changed.

"This is not surprising," she wrote. "I was barely eighteen when I came here, and what have I not been through! First principle: never to let one's self be beaten down by persons or events." There would be many "persons and events" later in her life that would try to beat her down, but Manya Sklodowska had already learned not to give up.

CHAPTER FIVE

The Turning Point

At the beginning of the summer of 1889, Manya's freedom had finally arrived! Her contract with the Zorawskis was completed. Once again she took the seven hour journey back to Warsaw. How she looked forward to seeing her beloved father again! She missed Warsaw, too, especially the part of town called Old City, where she had been born. The tall houses there were very fancy. Under their sloping, red-tiled roofs were the carved faces of different saints. Signs for inns and shops were decorated with the figures of animals.

Manya stayed in Warsaw for only a short time. Almost immediately she went on to her next employers, a family who was vacationing on the Baltic Sea. That fall, the family returned to spend the winter in Warsaw. Her new employers treated her well, and her job was not difficult.

Then, in March of the next year, she received a letter from Bronya, who was in Paris. Bronya had hopes of marrying a Pole named Casimir Dluski. He was a fellow medical student in Paris. They were going to stay in France a little longer while he finished his studies. Bronya wrote, "Now you, my little Manya, you must make something of your life sometime. If you can get together a few hundred rubles this year, you can come to Paris next year and live with us." Bronya wanted her to enroll at the Sorbonne and live with them for a year. After that, the Dluskis hoped to return to Poland, and Manya would stay on by herself in Paris. Bronya was sure Mr. Sklodowski would send Manya money for her education.

At last Manya's dream to further her education could come true! But what did she decide to do instead? She remained in Poland! She was sure that her father wanted her to stay there with him. She wrote to Bronya, "I believe our plan of living together next year is close to his heart, and he clings to it." She had also promised her sister Hela that she would help her find a job in Warsaw. Her sense of duty to her father and sister was too strong.

Bronya argued, but Manya's mind was made up. She decided to finish her governess job, and then stay at home in Warsaw for a year. If she lived with her father, she could save her money and then, *maybe*, she would be able to go to Paris.

In the meantime, while she was in Warsaw, she returned to the Floating University. By this time, the Floating University had a laboratory! It was on Krakovski Boulevard, in a tiny, one story building with tiny windows. One had to walk through a courtyard planted with lilacs to reach the lab. A cousin of Manya's, Joseph Boguski, directed the lab which everyone called "The Museum of Industry and Agriculture." It wasn't really a museum. The Poles had given it that name so the Russians wouldn't know that it was part of the secret Floating University.

Manya did not have much time to work in this laboratory. She usually went there only in the evenings after dinner or on Sunday. She usually had to work alone. Nevertheless, she tried to reproduce the experiments described in her physics and chemistry books. Years later, she wrote about her first experiences in a laboratory. She said she had learned that this kind of work was slow and difficult. But, she wrote, "I developed my taste for experimental research during these first trials."

She loved to hold the glass test tubes, the balances, the electrometers. She taught herself how to use a blowpipe and carbon-block, and how to turn cloudy liquids into clear ones. When she went home at night, all the wonderful things in the laboratory stayed in her dreams.

Being in the laboratory only made her desire to go to the Sorbonne ever stronger. She *had* to learn even more than she was learning now! Oh, how she wanted to go, but she was torn. She wanted to make her father happy. She felt she could only do that if she stayed with him in Warsaw. And there was Hela, too. Manya was trying to find her a job. Her family responsibilities fought with her longing for a university education. For the time being, her family duty won.

In September, 1891, Manya went on a vacation in the Carpathian Mountains. While she was there she met Casimir Zorawski again. She realized she still cared for him. Was he ready to marry her now? The rich, handsome Casimir still cared for the pretty, but poor, Manya, but he was too afraid of his parents' disapproval. He didn't have the courage to go against them and marry someone who was below his social class. In despair, Manya told him, "If you can't see a way to clear up our situation, it is not for me to teach you." This time, she threw away all hopes she'd had that they would marry. Sick at heart, she renewed her vows not to fall in love again.

When Manya came back from that vacation, she had changed her mind about going to Paris. She would do it! She had saved enough money for the Sorbonne. Hela and her father were doing well. Besides, she wouldn't be gone for long. There was no reason for her not to go. Her main concern was that Bronya was going to have a baby, and she didn't want to be in the way. But Bronya insisted that there was plenty of room for Manya.

So, in the fall of 1891, Manya boarded the train, and headed for her dream. She had already sent her mattress, blankets, sheets, and towels. A big wooden trunk held her clothes. Since she was traveling as cheaply as she could, she packed her own food for the three day trip. She even took a folding chair, since the train didn't offer seating!

Her father was there to see her off. How painful it was to leave him. At the train station, she told him, "I shall not be away long—two years, three at the most. As soon as I have finished my studies, I'll come back. We shall live together and never be separated again."

Her father smiled at his favorite daughter. He said in a hoarse voice, "Yes, my little Manyusya. Come back quickly. Work hard. Good luck!"

CHAPTER SIX

A French Education

Paris! The Sorbonne! How excited Manya was! Courses would begin on November 3. She had exchanged her hard earned rubles for French money, called francs. She used francs to pay her registration fee at the Sorbonne. Not only was her money now French, but so was her first name! When she registered, she used the French version of her name, which was Marie. From then on, she called herself Marie. Little Manya existed only in memories.

Marie's last name, Sklodowska, was hard for the French to pronounce, but she wouldn't allow anyone to call her by her first name. So, for a long time, her classmates didn't call her anything. Marie was timid, but she sat as close to the front of her classes as possible. She didn't want to miss anything her professors said. They were very impressive, dressed in their black suits and white ties. The problem was that, while the French had trouble understanding Polish, Marie was having trouble understanding French. Even though she sat at the front of the rooms, she missed too much valuable information. This would never do! Marie set out to learn French. And she did. She worked until she knew French better than the French did! There was hardly even any Polish accent left.

Marie may have learned enough French, but she was still lacking in science. All the studying she had done on her own could not equal what French students were taught in preparatory schools. At the Sorbonne all the other students knew much more about science than she did. Marie spent hours and hours working to catch up. Nothing was going to keep her from her dream, which was to earn the title "Master of Science." When she had her degree, she knew she'd be ready to return to Poland and teach Polish children. That was still her intention, to be a teacher.

To be in Paris at the Sorbonne was her greatest joy. All her years of waiting and saving had been worth it. Never had she been so happy.

Her home with Bronya and Casimir was full of love. Casimir had accepted his sister-in-law into his home as part of his family. He was a person who was full of life and gaiety. He wanted life to be full of excitment, even if no one had any money. He'd organize a party to go to the theater in the cheapest seats. If there was no money for tickets, he'd invite friends to his home. Other young Polish couples knew that they could always go to the Dluskis' for some fun. There would be piano playing, refreshments, lots of talk and laughter.

Marie began to have problems with the loud gaiety in the evenings. That was the only time she had to study.

Casimir would come to her room and bring her downstairs to join the fun. He insisted that she come to the "concerts."

Marie felt that Bronya and Casimir worked hard all day as doctors, and they deserved to relax after work. But Marie could not relax. She had spent years of sacrifice so she could attend the university. With her goal finally in sight, she was not about to let Casimir, no matter how nice he was, *waste* her time. She had *studying* to do. He would have to leave her alone. But he wouldn't.

Finally Marie sat down with her sister and her brother-in-law to talk it over. She decided that she would have to move to her own place. The Dluskis hated the idea, but Marie was firm. She had to have peace and quiet in which to study. Besides, the Dluskis' apartment was an hour away from the Sorbonne. Marie felt she was spending too much money on the bus trips to and from the university. She found a small room that was close to the Sorbonne and its library and laboratories. It was in the Latin Quarter, where many students lived.

Now that she was out on her own, she had to watch her money very closely. There would be no more free room and board. Marie began living like so many poor students in those days. There were hundreds just like her who lived in poverty just to get their precious education. Marie had to spread out her savings. She decided she would have to live on three francs a day. Those three francs were to pay for her rent, meals, clothes, papers and books, and fees at the university. She was willing to be frugal. Her education was more important than anything, including taking care of herself. Marie began to skip meals. Sometimes she'd just forget to eat. When she did remember, she might have only some bread and tea. Once in a while she'd have an egg. The truth is, Marie didn't know how to cook—not even soup! She didn't want to waste her precious francs on expensive foods like meat. And she certainly wasn't going to waste her precious time learning to cook. Each month she grew thinner and pushed herself harder. Often, she'd stay up studying until two or three o'clock in the morning.

The places she rented were cheap, and bare. In her search for peace and quiet, she tried several different rooms. Finally, she ended up in an attic, at the top of six flights of stairs. It, too, was bare and had to be furnished with Marie's own things. Here's all that she owned: an iron folding bed, a mattress, a stove, a white wooden table, a kitchen chair, a washbasin, and an oil lamp. She also had an alcohol heater on which she cooked her meals—when she did! For extra seating, in case someone visited, she had an old brown trunk which she used as her chest of drawers.

In winter, this attic would get so cold, ice would form on top of the water in the basin. Marie had a coal stove to heat the room, but she didn't want to spend much money on coal. Many times she wouldn't even light the stove. To keep warm, she would dress in several layers of clothing. Then she would lie down on her bed and cover herself with her blanket and coats.

Eventually, the lack of food and sleep made her

Marie studying.

weak. One day she fainted right in front of a friend. The Dluskis were told, and Casimir arrived as fast as he could. He found the pale, thin, young woman studying as if nothing had happened!

He looked Marie over carefully with his medically trained eye. He was not at all happy with what he saw. Then he noticed that her dishes were very clean, and that there was *nothing* in the room to eat but *tea*.

"What did you eat today?" he demanded.

"Today? I don't know. I had lunch a while ago."

Casimir was suspicious. "What did you eat?" he asked again.

"Some cherries and . . . and all sorts of things," Marie stammered.

Marie couldn't fool her brother-in-law. He found out that all she'd eaten in two days were some radishes and a few cherries. He also got Marie to confess that she'd been working until three o'clock in the morning! Not enough food *or* rest! Casimir was disgusted. He packed her off to his house so that he and his wife could build up Marie's strength. As soon as she arrived, Marie was forced to sit down and eat a huge steak and a plateful of fried potatoes. After a few days she was well fed and rested and ready to return to her own room. The Dluksis made her promise she'd take better care of herself. She promised, and she really meant it. But soon she was, once again, forgetting to eat and sleep. There was only one thing Marie Sklodowska remembered to do at the Sorbonne, and that was to study.

Marie loved working in the physics laboratory at the Sorbonne. She would rather have been there than anyplace else in the world. Long ago, she had wanted to play with her father's "Phy-sics app-a-ra-tus," and now she could. Now she was even performing experiments. She didn't think she could ever be happier.

Marie had decided to get two degrees instead of one. In addition to her degree in physics, she also wanted one in mathematics. The only problem was that meant she'd have to stay in Paris longer. She felt badly because she knew her father was expecting her to return to Poland. She couldn't bear to tell him of her decision. Mr. Sklodowski did not know his little Manya was staying for a second degree until Bronya told him in a letter.

In 1893, Marie achieved her first goal. She received her Masters in physics. All those nights of studying late had been worth it. That July, she was among the crowd of students and their families waiting to hear the names of students who had passed their physics exam. The top student's name was read first. It was Marie Sklodowska! She was at the head of her class! No one knew whether she was pleased or not, for Marie's face showed no emotion. She simply rushed back to her room to pack for her return to Poland.

Marie spent the entire summer in Poland. All her relatives were shocked at how thin she'd become. All the tastiest Polish foods were cooked for Marie. Her family wanted to fatten her up before she returned to the Sorbonne in November. But back in Paris, she lived just as she had before.

This time, though, she was able to go to the university without taking money from her father. Through a Polish student at the Sorbonne, Marie won the "Alexandrovitch Scholarship." It was for students of merit who wanted to study outside of Poland. It was 600 rubles! A wonderful sum. Marie certainly deserved the money, but she was not about to spend it quickly. She decided to spread it out so she could live in Paris for 15 months.

Most students just took the money, spent it on their education, and went on to their careers. As usual, Marie did something extra. A few years later, she had saved enough money to repay the Alexandrovitch Foundation. She wanted some other poor Pole to get a scholarship, too.

CHAPTER SEVEN

Changes

In 1894, Marie was asked to do some scientific work for pay. She did a study on how magnetic different kinds of steel were. She was grateful for this chance, but in order to perform her experiments, she had to use large equipment. Unfortunately, the equipment was too large for the room at the Sorbonne where she would work. A fellow Pole named Joseph Kovalski was in Paris for some scientific meetings. During a visit with him, Marie told him about her problem.

He said, "I have an idea. I know a scientist who works in the School of Physics and Chemistry. Perhaps he might have a workroom available. In any case, he could give you some advice. Come and have tea tomorrow evening with my wife and me. I will ask the young man to come. You probably know his name. It is Pierre Curie."

The next evening Marie and Pierre Curie met for the first time. Pierre was 35 years old then, but Marie thought he seemed much younger. Later, she described their meeting. She said she was struck by his clear gaze. She liked the fact that he didn't seem overly concerned with his appearance. And his slow, simple way of speaking, along with his smile, inspired her confidence.

Pierre Curie.

Pierre was also impressed with Marie. At last, he had found a woman who could talk intelligently about his first love, science. Years before this meeting, Pierre had written in his diary, "Women of genius are rare." He may not have realized that he had just met one of those rare women of genius.

What he did realize, however, was that he wanted to see Marie again. He found the charming, young woman so easy to talk to. She didn't flirt with him like many other young ladies. He admired her high, curved forehead, her blonde hair, and her grace. There was something that greatly attracted him to this woman. He knew that she was a Polish student studying in Paris. He asked Marie a question that he wasn't really sure why he was asking. "Are you going to remain in France always?"

"Certainly not," she replied crisply. "This summer, if I succeed in my master's examination, I shall go back to Warsaw. I should like to come back here in the autumn, but I don't know whether I'll have the means to do so. Later on I shall be a teacher in Poland, and I shall try to be useful. Poles have no right to abandon their country."

These were forceful words. Marie's ideals were high. Marie deeply loved her country, and she wanted it to be free. For her part, she would use her education to help bring about that freedom.

Pierre hated the idea of such a brilliant mind going outside the field of science. In the next few weeks, he saw Marie many times, often in her laboratory. He asked to visit her, and she gave him her permission. He gave her a copy of his latest publication. He had autographed it, "To Miss Sklodovska, with the respect and friendship of the author."

That summer, Marie passed her examination, and received her Masters Degree in mathematics. She prepared to return to Warsaw, but Pierre didn't want her to stay there. He told her she should return to Paris in the fall; that she "had no right to abandon science."

He wanted her to become a scientist rather than a

teacher. He didn't see any sense in getting involved with politics.

He also wanted very badly for Marie to marry him. But she returned to Poland. She would only give him the promise that they could be "friends." And she would give him no assurance that she'd come back to Paris in the fall. All summer he wrote her many letters trying to convince her to come back. He always signed them, "Your devoted friend." Sometimes his letters appealed to her through science. Sometimes Pierre expressed his desire for them to further their friendship. Pierre Curie had at last found a woman he greatly admired, and he didn't want her to slip out of his life.

"It would be a fine thing," Pierre wrote to Marie, "for us to pass our lives near each other, hypnotized by our dreams."

Pierre hoped Marie's dream was the same as his—a life devoted to science. He did not believe she should spend her time trying to change Poland. He felt that even if people could change society, the change might just be for the worse. He told Marie that only through science could they hope to change the world. He was sure that whatever was achieved in science, no matter how small, *would* benefit humankind.

There were many letters like this, but Marie resisted changing her plans. She had had her dream too long to abandon it so quickly. She had never planned to be a scientist, but a *teacher*. When Pierre's older brother, Jacques, was shown Marie's picture, he said, "she has a very decided look, even stubborn."

Pierre often saw Marie in her laboratory.

Finally Pierre got *one* answer from Marie he wanted. She was going to come back to Paris in the fall. She was not returning to marry him. She was going to work on her doctorate at the Sorbonne.

Throughout the next year Pierre didn't give up. He offered to find a job in Poland if she was so determined to return there. He went to Bronya and asked for her help. He took Marie to visit his parents in Sceaux, a southern suburb of Paris where they lived. It took 10 months of constant appeal, but finally, on July 26, 1895, his persistence paid off. Marie Sklodowska, that young woman who had vowed never to fall in love again, married Pierre Curie. The couple had the blessings of both families. Marie adored Pierre's parents, and they loved her, too. Mr. Sklodowski and Hela came from Poland to attend the wedding in Sceaux. The Dluskis were there, too. Marie's brother Joseph wrote that it was better for her to be happy in Paris than unhappy in Poland. He sent her a "thousand kisses," and wishes for "happiness, joy, and success."

Marie did not want to make a big occasion out of her wedding. She didn't want a fancy, special dress either. Marie was too practical. She never spent money on herself. She did accept a present of a wedding dress from Bronya's mother-in-law. But she had asked, "Please make it practical and dark, so that I can put in on afterwards to go to the laboratory."

Marie's decision to marry Pierre caused her some pain, as well as joy. To marry him meant she had to stay in France. She knew she would never return to her beloved Poland to carry out her dream of helping it. However, a stronger desire now held her. She wrote her old friend Kazia that it was sad for her to have to stay forever in Paris. However, she and Pierre were deeply in love, so what could she do? They could not bear being separated.

The couple was really very well suited for each other. Although they were from different countries, they were both dedicated to science. Pierre didn't care about collecting a lot of possessions, and neither did Marie. For them, the most important thing in the world was science. Science was making great progress when the Curies lived. They felt that pure scientific experimentation was of extreme importance to humankind. This dedication to the same ideal, and their strong love for each other, made their marriage a very good one.

They began with a honeymoon on bicycles. Marie had bought them with money given them for a wedding present. They toured the French countryside, then returned to Paris in October. They travelled over country roads, stopping at whatever inn they happened to discover. Sometimes they would take off across a field or nap beside a stream. This trip together created between them a strong emotional bond. They began their life together in complete harmony. Their tiny three-room apartment had few furnishings. They used one of the rooms as a study. It held a desk, two chairs, a lamp, and some books. There was nothing to dust or straighten. There was no cleaning to rob Marie of precious time needed for her scientific experimentation.

Marie and Pierre on their honeymoon.

The Curies settled down to their individual scientific experiments. Pierre was researching the structure of crystals. Marie, besides working toward her doctorate, was completing her study of steel. The Curies had met each other through science. And it was to science that they dedicated their life together.

CHAPTER EIGHT

A Surprising Discovery

For the next two years, Marie continued her study of the magnetization of steel. She also worked on organizing her household. She taught herself to cook quick, simple meals. She still didn't want eating to rob her of precious time that belonged to scientific research. She continued to work toward her doctorate degree. At that time, no woman in Europe had ever received a doctorate. There was only one other woman besides Marie who was even working toward the high degree. She lived in Germany. So Marie was trying to accomplish a first—for herself, and for women.

These years brought her another first. Her first daughter, Irene, was born on September 12, 1897. The baby was delivered by Pierre's father, who was a doctor. Two months later, in a letter to her father, Marie called Irene her "little queen." She was a beautiful baby, but she had a bad appetite. Marie was eventually forced to get a nurse for her.

Marie had been quite sick throughout most of the pregnancy. It had prevented her from doing her work as quickly as she wanted. Still, this same year, she finished the study of steel. The project had taken three years to complete. She used her fee to repay the scholarship she'd received from the Alexandrovich Foundation. The secretary for the foundation was very surprised. No one had ever repaid them before!

There were heartaches during those two years, also. Shortly after the birth of Irene, Pierre's mother died of cancer. Doctor Curie moved in with his son and daughter-in-law after his wife died, and became a great companion for Irene. This was a good thing, since Irene's mother and father spent so much time in the laboratory.

Before Marie could earn her doctorate she had to write a research paper, or thesis. First, however, she had to pick a subject for her thesis. It was a big choice to make. The thesis had to be her own, original work. With Pierre, Marie began going over the most recent work in physics done by others. After studying the work done so far, they decided what Marie's thesis would be. It was based on a scientific discovery made by a man named Henri Becquerel.

In 1896, Becquerel had published a scientific paper announcing an important discovery. He had found that uranium salts gave off rays that were similar to X rays. X rays are invisible electromagnetic rays that can pass through solid objects. They had been discovered a year earlier by a German scientist named Roentgen. They were called "X" because that was the symbol for the unknown. Where this invisible radiation came from was not yet known. Mssr. Becquerel had taken a photographic plate.

Then he had wrapped it completely in black paper, so that no light could reach it. He put some uranium salts on the paper-covered plate, and put the plate in a drawer and shut it. He left it there for a while. When he pulled out the plate and unwrapped the paper, he discovered something that shocked him. Even though no light had gotten to the plate, there was an impression on it. What had caused the impression? He knew there was only one answer. Somehow the uranium must have caused it, but he wasn't really sure how. In his paper he explained the impression as being caused by "rays of unknown origin."

The Curies read Becquerel's paper about the impression made by uranium salts. They knew that energy had allowed the uranium salts to give off rays. But where had the energy come from? They decided that Marie would find out for her thesis.

The next task was to find a place where Marie could work. Pierre went to the School of Physics and Chemistry where he taught. He asked the director for a place in which Marie could carry on her experiments. The only studio available was a small one on the ground floor of the school. The glassed-in room had been used partly as a store room and partly as a machine shop. It was not a good place in which to carry out experiments using electricity. The room was very damp and often quite cold. The dampness and cold were Marie's enemies, for they prevented her tools from being accurate. Sometimes it was only 44 degrees in that room! Marie would record the temperature in her notebook. Then she would follow the figure with ten exclamation points to show how disgusted she was.

The damp, drafty room was bad for Marie's experiments, and bad for Marie's health. She had been ill for much of the previous year because of her pregnancy, and she was still weak. As usual, Marie was not about to let her physical condition get in her way. She set about conducting her experiments without thinking about herself. She was concerned about those mysterious rays. From where did they come?

First she decided to find out how much energy the uranium gave off. She used a method her husband and his brother had devised years before. It was called the piezoelectric effect in quartz. The brothers had discovered that quartz changed shape if an electrical charge was run through it. They would measure how much the quartz had changed. Then they could figure out how much electrical current had been used. This method could measure only very weak amounts of electricity, but it was very precise. Using this method, Marie began measuring the strength of the rays of different amounts of uranium.

At the end of several weeks of experimentation, Marie discovered something very interesting. The larger the piece of uranium she had, the stronger the rays it gave off. It didn't matter if the uranium salts were dry, wet, in lumps, or in powdered form.

At the time that Marie made this discovery she didn't realize how important it was. Scientists thought that these rays were caused by molecules changing shapes, or by atoms forming new molecules. But Marie's experiment didn't show that happening. No matter what chemicals she added to the uranium, the strength of the rays was the same. The only time the amount of the rays increased or decreased, was when the amount of uranium was changed. "Why?" Marie wondered. She finally came up with one explanation. The rays had to come from the *atoms* that made up the uranium molecules themselves!

Now Marie was excited. If uranium could produce rays like that, could there be any other elements that did the same thing? She decided to find out. First, she would collect samples and test them, too. She was too poor to simply go out and buy pieces of substances to test. So she went through the school and begged people to give her whatever they had. She collected all kinds of metals and minerals. She tested them all to see if they gave off rays like uranium. She discovered that an element called thorium could. She decided she needed to give these "rays of unknown origin" a name. She called them "radiation."

Even though Marie had discovered that both uranium and thorium emitted radiation, she still didn't know how they did it.

Marie had tested two more substances for radioactivity. One was called pitchblende. The other was called chalcolite. Both of them were minerals that were known to contain some uranium. Marie measured the rays given off by pitchblende. The radiation was much stronger than it should have been for the small amount of uranium it contained. The radiation in pitchblende was four times as strong as it was in pure uranium. The chalcolite was two times stronger than pure uranium.

"It must be a mistake in my experiment," Marie told herself. So she repeated her test. The results were the same. Both of the substances were far more radioactive than they should be. Where did the extra radiation come from? It was a puzzle. Marie thought she knew the answer, and she was very excited!

Marie's problem was similar to finding out what is in a chocolate cake. You know you taste more than chocolate in it. So you would decide that something else in the cake is causing the other tastes. How could you find out what is responsible for the other tastes? You would have to determine what ingredients are in the cake to have the answer. This is what Marie thought. She realized there was *something else* in the pitchblende and chalcolite that was also radioactive!

Marie had already tested all *known* chemical elements. She knew they were not responsible for the radiation. There weren't any more elements to test. So that left only one other explanation for the source of the excess radiation. It had to be caused by a brand new, so far *undiscovered*, element!

CHAPTER NINE

More Discoveries

Pierre and Marie were very excited by Marie's discovery. Marie wanted to share her new findings with Bronya. When she went to see her sister, she told her, "You know, Bronya, the radiation that I couldn't explain comes from a new chemical element. The element is there and I've got to find it. We are sure! The physicists we have spoken to believe we have made an error. But I am convinced that I am not mistaken."

Scientists have a habit of questioning everything. They don't believe what they see the first time. And they still hadn't seen this new element at all! In spite of the scientist's doubts, on April 12, 1898, Marie made an official announcement. She stated that she believed there was a new radioactive element in pitchblende ore. Then she set out to prove her theory.

Fascinated by his wife's discovery, Pierre now joined Marie in her research. His dream of working side by side with Marie had finally come true. They would work together to find the new element in pitchblende.

At that time, scientists thought they already knew all of the elements found in pitchblende. The Curies decided that the new element must be very small, if no one knew about it. First, they separated the known elements out of the pitchblende. They treated the pitchblende with chemicals that would attract or dissolve the known elements. This method would finally leave only their new, unknown element.

By June of 1898, Marie believed her element was contained in an element called bismuth. Bismuth is highly metallic, and has been used in cosmetics, medicine, and printing. Now, she thought, how could she separate the mysterious element out of bismuth? She mixed a special solution in a test tube. Some of the solids in the tube settled to the bottom. As Marie looked at the solid, she wondered if this was her new element. She measured its radioactivity and was more certain. In her notebook she wrote: *150 times more active than uranium.* She underlined her entry because she was so excited about this discovery.

Pierre then took some of the solid and put it in a glass tube. He started to heat it. Pretty soon a thin, black powder formed on the sides of the glass. After scraping the powder from the tube, he and Marie measured its radioactivity. It was very strong. They produced a sample that was 330 times more radioactive than uranium.

Soon they discovered this first radioactive sample was actually *two* elements. In their notebook, they wrote, "We have found a second radioactive substance, entirely different from the first." So they had not one, but *two* new elements! When they were finally able to separate one of them Pierre turned to Marie. He said, "You will have to name it."

Marie immediately thought of Poland. She wanted

Pierre Curie measuring radium.

to honor her country in some way. She asked her husband, "Could we call it 'polonium'?" So that's what they did.

The other unknown element they named "the other."

They officially announced the discovery of "polonium" that July.

After the announcement, they went on a much needed vacation. Pierre was suffering from pains in his legs. The doctors told him it was rheumatism. Marie's fingertips were beginning to develop sores. No one knew that radiation sickness could cause these problems. These two had been working with radioactive substances for months. They didn't know that their scientific work was making them sick. They just thought they were very tired. So off Pierre and Marie went with their little Irene and their bicycles. They rented a house out in the country in a little town called Auroux. They climbed hills, bathed in rivers, and rode their bikes to nearby towns. They always talked about their work, about "the other."

Soon after the Curies returned, Bronya and Casimir moved away from Paris. They went back to Poland to open a sanitorium for tuberculosis patients. After they left, Marie felt terribly alone. She wrote Bronya, "You can't imagine the hole you have made in my life. With you two, I have lost everything I clung to in Paris, except my husband and child."

Back in Paris, the Curies continued to work in the laboratory. Now they were trying to separate out "the other." They used the same chemical methods as before.

The Curies vacationing in the country.

By the end of November, they had removed both polonium and bismuth from the black powder. What was
left was "the other!" They measured it's radioactivity. It
turned out to be 900 times higher than uranium! Now
they were sure they had done it! They had separated the
other element from all other known radioactive substances. It, alone, was responsible for the huge amount
of radiation. On December 26, 1898, they announced
their discovery in a journal called the *Proceedings of the*

Academy. This journal was put out by a special scientific organization.

In the journal, they described their experiments and the results. They listed all the reasons why they believed they had found a new element. And they gave their new element a name, radium.

In the months to come they would find out more about this element, radium. Unfortunately, not all of it would be good.

CHAPTER TEN

Four Hard Years

Wh   hen Marie and Pierre announced their discovery of radium, not all the scientists believed them. The scientists wanted the Curies to produce "pure" radium. They wanted to be able to weigh it, to see it, and to touch it, if possible. They wanted proof before they would accept radium's existence. They demanded that the Curies isolate some "pure" radium, then calculate its atomic weight. The atomic weight of an element is simply the weight of one of its atoms. The atomic weight must be determined before an element can be listed on the Periodic Table of Elements. The Periodic Table is a listing of the atomic weights (or, today, the atomic number) of elements.

The Curies really had hard work ahead of them. By now they knew that the amount of radium in pitchblende was extremely small. In fact, it was a lot smaller than they'd first suspected. They had been working in pounds of pitchblende, but that wouldn't be enough. Out of all those pounds of pitchblende, they had gotten only a tiny amount of radium and polonium. They'd need *tons* of pitchblende in order to get enough radium and polonium to weigh! But where could they get it? And once they got it, where would they work with it? The glassed-in shed was much too small! They tried to find a place at the Sorbonne, but none was available. Again, they approached the School of Physics where Pierre taught and were offered a place to work. But what a place! It was a drafty, leaky shed in back of the school, with a dirt floor. Inside, there were only some kitchen tables, a blackboard, and an old cast iron stove with a rusty pipe. The shed was considered abandoned, and for good reason. No one would want to work there. But the Curies had no choice.

Now that they had a place in which to work, they had to obtain the pitchblende. They had a small savings, and were prepared to spend it on the ore. But pitchblende was extremely expensive. They didn't have enough money to buy as much as they needed. However, they learned that a mine in Bavaria removed uranium from pitchblende. The residue, or what was left over, contained exactly what the Curies wanted—polonium and radium. What's more, the residue was a lot cheaper than the pitchblende.

They asked the owners of the mine if they could buy some of the residue at a reasonable price. The mine owners were only too glad to get rid of what they considered garbage. If those two crazy French scientists wanted it, they could have a ton of it! All they'd have to do was pay for its transportation.

The Curies were delighted. One day a huge coal wagon arrived in front of the School of Physics. It was loaded with sacks and sacks of the pitchblende. Marie ran out to greet the truck, opened one of the sacks, and happily sank her hands deep into the residue. Here, at last, was the material she needed for her work. Out of this, she was sure, she could get pure radium!

Marie and Pierre began the work that would take them four years to complete. They did it under the most awful conditions imaginable. In summer, the shed was like a hot house because of its glass roof. The glass panes weren't sealed well. When it rained, the water dripped in all over their experiments! When the weather turned cold, the useless stove warmed the Curies only if they stood right next to it. If they took two steps away from the stove, they were shivering once again.

There was no chimney for ventilation, either. Since their chemical processes gave off toxic gasses, the Curies had to keep windows open—all year 'round! Sometimes they simply worked outside in the nearby courtyard. If it rained, they would have to run inside, hauling their equipment with them. These terrible conditions certainly didn't improve the Curies's health. Marie was beginning to have bouts of tuberculosis. Fortunately, she was never as sick as her mother had been.

It was in this drafty shed, that the Curies worked from 1898 to 1902. The first year they separated radium and polonium out of the pitchblende. Then they studied these elements' radiation. Scientists had believed that radioactive substances eventually destroyed themselves. They thought the amount of radiation given off became smaller in the process. The Curies discovered that the radioactivity of radium was constant; its strength did *not* weaken. This was confusing to them.

Pierre in process of extracting radium.

They decided to divide the work. Pierre concentrated on finding out what made up radium. Marie did the back-breaking work of separating radium from the pitchblende residue. She would mix the pitchblende residue with chemicals in a large vat, then she would boil the mixture and stir it for hours with an iron rod as thick as her arm!

One might assume that the Curies were absolutely miserable in this horrible place. Yet, years later Marie

The shed where radium was discovered.

wrote, "It was in this miserable old shed, that the best and happiest years of our life were spent, entirely consecrated to work."

In 1900, the Curies were made an offer that would have gotten them out of the drafty, damp shed. The University of Geneva, Switzerland, wanted these two scientists to come work for them. They even offered them the chance to set up their own laboratory. Immediately, Pierre accepted the offer, and he and Marie went to visit the university. It would be the answer to their dreams if they could have a brand new laboratory. They realized it would take time to move their household to Switzerland. Then more time would be spent setting up the new laboratory. Marie's work would have to stop while they moved. After much discussion, they decided that even a short interruption was not a good idea. These two dedicated individuals didn't want to stop their work. It had begun to own them, body and soul! Pierre wrote to the university. He explained that he was sorry, but they had changed their minds.

They still needed extra money to help support their family. Pierre took a job at the Sorbonne, and Marie took a job teaching at the Higher Normal School for Girls in Sevres. The new jobs brought in extra income. They also made extra demands on the Curies's energy and time.

When Marie began teaching at the school, she lost 15 pounds. Pierre sometimes had to go to bed because of the pain caused by attacks of rheumatism. People who knew them were alarmed. But the Curies were not concerned. They told their friends, "We do rest, and we go on vacations." Their friends pointed out that they went only in the summer. And then they rode on bicycles the whole time! That was *not* exactly a restful vacation.

In addition to her hard work in school and the lab, Marie tried to be a good mother. She always insisted on bathing Irene, and later her sister Eve. She never allowed anyone else to do this. She described their life to Bronya in 1899: "Our life is always the same. We work a lot, but we sleep well. The evenings are taken up by caring for the child. In the morning, I dress her and give her her food, then I can generally go out at about nine."

When she went out at nine o'clock, it was to teach at the school in Sevres. After classes, she'd go to the shed where she'd spend hours stirring her boiling mixture. It took her longer than it would have to extract the pure radium because the shed was so poorly sealed. Dirt and rain would fall through the roof of the shed. They would mix with the radium Marie collected, making it useless. She would have to start all over again. Pierre was ready to stop for a while, until a better place could be found. But Marie was stubborn. She refused to halt their research.

Their fascination with this element went on for months, and then years. They would talk about the radium like curious children.

"I wonder what IT will be like, what IT will look like," Marie would say to Pierre. "What form do you imagine IT will take?"

"I don't know," he would reply. "I should like it to have a very beautiful color."

In May of 1902, Marie's family in Warsaw wrote that her father was very ill. He had gallstones and had needed an operation. Immediately, she boarded a train for Poland. When she arrived, Mr. Sklodowski was already dead. Marie was not able to see him one last time. She was so upset that she wept over his coffin and begged his forgiveness for disappointing him. She'd always felt guilty for not returning to Warsaw to live with her father. She felt she had broken the promise she'd made to him so many years before.

Sad and even thinner, Marie returned to Paris in September and resumed her work. By the following month, she had finished writing her doctorate thesis. It was the results of her work on the purification of radium. Even though Marie felt she had disappointed her father, she really had not. He had lived long enough to know that she had achieved her goal. Six days before he died, he had written to her happily, "And now you are in possession of salts of pure radium!"

Yes, her persistence had been rewarded. Four years earlier, the Curies had announced that they suspected radium existed. Now, Marie had produced one tenth of a gram of pure radium. To get it, she treated *eight tons* of pitchblende residue! She determined it had an atomic weight of 225 (although now it is recognized as 226). At last, scientists would have to accept that radium did indeed exist.

The Curies kept several glass bottles of the pure radium in their lab. One night, after they had come home from the lab, Marie suggested they return. They told Pierre's father where they were going. Then, arm in arm, they walked back.

Pierre unlocked the lab door and started to light the lamps. Marie stopped him.

"Don't light the lamps," she said. Then she asked, "Do you remember when you told me, 'I should like radium to have a beautiful color'? Look. Look!" Marie told him.

In awe, they went into the darkened laboratory. Marie sat on a chair in the middle of the room. Pierre stood behind her. They gazed in wonder at their radium. On the shelves and tables, the radium glowed a beautiful blue in the darkness. It seemed as if they were surrounded by blue fireflies. It was an evening that Marie never forgot.

For the Curies, this night was enough of a reward. They did not wish to become rich from their scientific research. They lived during a time when science was dedicated to research. This research was done so that the results could be added to existing scientific knowledge. Scientists did not worry if nothing practical came from their work. A scientist was only supposed to find new knowledge for science. The Curies felt this way. Years later, others would discover ways to use their knowledge of radium and radiation. But that was not the reason the Curies had worked so hard.

This wonderful radium delighted them with its blue glow. At this point they didn't realize it could also be a deadly force. The Curies had kept careful notes on their progress in the shed. From 1897 to 1900, they wrote everything in three notebooks. Today, those notebooks are still *locked up* because they are too radioactive for anyone to handle!

CHAPTER ELEVEN

Awards and Sorrows

The year 1902 was one of triumph for the Curies. They had proved the existence of radium. The next year did not begin as pleasantly. Marie became pregnant a second time, but lost the child. In a letter to Bronya, she wondered if she should blame the loss on her fatigue. Marie never really took good care of herself. She always felt she had strength for whatever she wanted to do. She simply ignored the times when her body complained.

There was another reason she might have lost the baby. At the time that she was pregnant, Marie was working with concentrated radium. It was kept in glass containers with cork or rubber stoppers. Radium releases a deadly gas called radon. At that time, no one knew that radon could pass through those containers. Marie's unborn child could have been harmed by radiation and radon.

That year, Bronya also lost a child. Pierre's attacks of rheumatism also began coming more often. Sometimes he'd lie in bed moaning all night! Through all this they both continued to teach classes. After school, they worked in the lab with their new-found radium.

Shortly after she lost her second child, Marie said to Pierre, "If one of us disappeared, the other should not survive. We can't exist without each other, can we?"

Pierre did not even want to think of living without Marie. But, he answered, "You are wrong. Whatever happens, even if one has to go on like a body without a soul, one must work just the same."

The Curies always put science ahead of themselves. After they discovered how to produce radium, famous scientists wanted information about radioactivity. Letters from all over the world flooded their home. They answered all of them generously. They could have made a lot of money from their knowledge. They could have patented, or claimed first rights to, their method of getting radium from pitchblende. Pierre and Marie talked about this. If they patented their process, it would mean extra income for their family. They certainly weren't rich and could use the money. Marie's answer was, "It is impossible. It would be contrary to the scientific spirit."

Pierre was happy with her answer. He said, "I think so, too." The two "pure" scientists wanted to share their work, not sell it.

One day, Pierre made an important discovery about radium. He found out that exposure to it could burn the skin. In the interests of science, he deliberately exposed his arm to radium radiation. He made notes about the burn: how it healed, how long it took, and what it looked like after it was healed. He put this information in a report to the Academy of Sciences.

About this same time, the scientist Henri Becquerel also made the same discovery. He was burned by a glass tube of radium he was carrying in his pocket. He wrote an article about the incident, too.

Because of these findings, Pierre began working with two professors named Charles Bouchard and V. Balthazard. They were both very high ranking medical men. Through their experiments, they discovered that radium could be used to destroy diseased cells. That meant they could cure growths, tumors, and certain forms of cancer. They named the process *Curietherapy*. The first doctors to practice Curietherapy used tubes of radium borrowed from the Curies. So the "purely" scientific discovery of the Curies was now useful to humankind.

Marie had finished writing the thesis she needed to get her doctoral degree. It was titled "Researchers on Radioactive Substances." Now she was required to submit her thesis to a number of important professors. The professors would read the thesis, and then ask her questions about her work. If she answered the questions well, she would be given her degree. After working on her doctorate for five years, Marie was ready to face the questioners.

The special occasion was June 5, 1903. Marie had bought a brand new dress—but not because she wanted to. Marie hardly ever bought herself new clothes. She was perfectly content to wear her dresses until they were shiny. Her sister Bronya had come to Paris for the event.

With her doctorate complete, Marie faces the questioners.

She insisted that Marie buy a new dress. They both went to a shop, where Bronya chose a long dress of silk and wool. But it was black like all of Marie's clothes. She wanted all her clothing to be dark, so it wouldn't show dirt from the laboratory.

The professors had already read her thesis. They questioned her a long time and were very impressed with her answers. They gave her the title of "Doctor of Physical Sciences." Marie did so well, the professors added "very honorable" to her title. There was not much fanfare at the ceremony. Only Pierre, Bronya, Dr. Curie, and some of Marie's students attended. But there was enough joy in that one room to fill a hundred.

After the formal ceremony, there was a gay dinner party given for Marie by a friend of the family. Late that evening, all the guests were sitting out in the garden talking. Pierre indicated his pride in his wife's accomplishment. He took from his pocket a small glass tube of radium. Then he held it up for all to admire. There in the darkness, everyone exclaimed over its blue glow.

More honors came to the Curies that year. In November, they were given the Davy Medal by the Royal Society of London. Pierre went to London alone to receive the medal. Marie was too ill to go with him. It was a beautiful gold medal. The Curies didn't know where to put it in their apartment. So they gave it to little Irene as a toy!

On December 10, 1903, the Curies were given the most important award they would ever receive together. It would prove to be the crowning point in their lives. The Academy of Science of Stockholm awarded them the Nobel Prize in Physics. The prize was shared by the Curies and Henri Becquerel for their discoveries in radioactivity. Becquerel first discovered that uranium gave off radiation. His finding led Marie to the discovery of radium. Sadly, the Curies were too sick to travel to Sweden and accept the award. The French Minister accepted it for them.

The Nobel Prize has always been an extremely important award. Those who receive it are greatly honored.

Along with the honor, the Curies were given 70,000 francs. Neither of these two scientists ever splurged on themselves. Some of the money went as loans or gifts to relatives. Some went into savings. Some was used to put a modern bathroom in their house and to wallpaper one of the rooms! Rarely did they spend the money on personal things, such as badly needed clothing. However, Marie insisted that Pierre leave his teaching job at the School of Physics. She felt he needed more time for rest.

Along with the honor of the Noble Prize, came something that the Curies did not like. It was a lot of attention. Letters that needed to be answered kept pouring in. The Curies simply didn't have the time to answer them all. They were constantly invited to banquets that they were forced to turn down. They hated the journalists wanting interviews and pictures. All they wanted to do was to be left alone to work.

Pierre resisted the attention of fame. He hated the idea that some people were made to seem more important than others. Marie shrank back from the honors and medals because she was so shy. Besides, she was too busy being a wife, mother, scientist, and teacher. She had no time to spare for all the things a "famous" woman was expected to do.

A year after they received the award, their lives were still hectic. Pierre wrote a friend, "I long for calmer days passed in a quiet place, where lectures will be forbidden and newspapermen persecuted."

Marie wrote her brother Joseph, "Always a hubbub. People are keeping us from work as much as they can."

That was true. Months later in the spring of 1904, they were still being sent hundreds of letters. They decided not to answer them, and to refuse to see visitors. The Curies were very private people with few close friends. All they wanted to do was work in peace.

CHAPTER TWELVE

Tragedy

At the end of 1904, Marie gave birth to her second daughter, Eve. Bronya came to help Marie after the delivery. Marie was so tired, she was depressed. She exclaimed to Bronya, "Why am I bringing this creature into the world? Existence is too hard. We ought not to inflict it on innocent ones." The exhaustion and depression she felt gradually went away as she became more rested. By February of 1905, she was back at her lab and in the school teaching.

In March, she wrote to her brother Joseph to report on how things were going with her enlarged family. "The children are growing well. Little Eve sleeps very little, and protests energetically if I leave her lying awake in her cradle. I carry her in my arms until she grows quiet. She does not resemble Irene. She has dark hair and blue eyes, whereas up to now Irene has rather light hair and green-brown eyes."

That summer the Curies went to Stockholm, Sweden, to give a lecture. This was the speech they would have given a year and a half earlier, when they received the Nobel Prize. They'd been too ill to go then. Pierre's health had been so bad over the past year, he hadn't worked at all. Finally he felt well enough to travel to

Sweden. On June 6th, Pierre stood before the Academy of Science of Stockholm. He spoke of the good radium could do. He also warned. "In criminal hands radium might become very dangerous. We might ask ourselves if humanity has anything to gain by learning the secrets of nature. Powerful explosives have permitted men to perform admirable work. They are also a terrible means of destruction in the hands of the great criminals who lead the peoples toward war."

These are wise words from a man of great vision. He may have had some warning, too. Five years earlier, a captain at the Ministry of War had asked him a question about radium. Could it be used to make gunsights and mine safety-catches that glowed in the dark? Then they could be used for night fighting. No doubt this had given Pierre a hint of the wrong ways his wife's discovery could be used.

Beginning in September, he had more frequent attacks of rheumatism. In despair, he wrote to a friend wondering if he'd *ever* be able to work in the lab again.

At last, the "hubbub," as Marie had called it, began to die down. Their lives settled into a kind of order. They began to make new friends. One was an American dancer, Loie Fuller, who lived in Paris. Another was the sculptor, Auguste Rodin, who is famous for his sculpture called "The Thinker." Life for the Curies was beginning to look normal.

In 1905, Pierre was nominated by the Academy of Science to become a member. Pierre was not impressed with such an honor. What he wanted was a good lab.

Then the Sorbonne offered him a professor's job. It was something he'd wanted for a long time. When he found out that no lab came with the job, he turned it down. The university offered to build him two labs. However, they would be on the Rue Cuvier, which was some distance from where he'd be teaching. Pierre was not happy about that, either. So the Sorbonne made him another offer, one he could hardly refuse. Pierre would have three co-workers, and one could be Marie. In fact, she could be chief of the laboratory work!

The Curies were very attached to the shed in which they'd labored for so many years. But they had to admit they were happy to leave it. After being shown the shed, a great German chemist wrote: "It was a cross between a stable and a potato-cellar. If I had not seen the worktable and chemical apparatus, I would have thought it was a practical joke."

The new lab was inconvenient, but the Curies went there every day after teaching. They were trying to determine how much radium a sample contained. To do this, they measured how much radioactivity the sample gave off.

The Curies were not healthy all the time, but they were very happy. They were doing what gave them the most pleasure. They were learning more about their radium. This was the most wonderful point in their lives together. Then the thing they'd always feared the most happened.

On the morning of April 19, 1906, Pierre was walking along the Rue Dauphine. The street was very crowded with carriages, wagons, pedestrians and cars. Apparently, Pierre decided to cross the street. He stepped out from behind a cab. Suddenly, he found himself right in the way of a horse-drawn wagon. Surprised, Pierre tried to grab onto one of the horses, to keep from slipping beneath the wagon wheels.

Pedestrians looking on cried, "Stop! Stop!" The driver yanked on the reins of the horses. But the wagon was too heavy to stop quickly. Pierre was knocked down, and his head was crushed by the great wheels. He was killed instantly.

When men came to the Curie apartment to tell Marie, she was at work. Pierre's father was at home, however. Upon learning of his son's death, he moaned, "What was he dreaming of this time?"

Marie returned home that day to learn that she was now a widow. She was only thirty-eight-years old. From that day on, she was a different woman. She was no longer gay and warm, but more like a robot. That first night after Pierre's death, she showed no outward signs of grief. The next day when she was alone in the room where Pierre's body had been placed, Pierre's brother Jacques came to be with her. There she was with the two Curie brothers, one dead and one alive. Only then did she weep until there were no tears left. Pierre was buried in Sceaux with his mother, in the family grave.

After his death, she wrote to Pierre in a diary. After Marie's death only her family was allowed to read this diary. Then they placed it in the National Library. No one was to read it until 1990. Eve Curie described the diary as sad and mournful, written on tearstained pages.

Pierre's coffin was placed in the grave. Marie placed some periwinkles from their garden and a picture of herself on the coffin. "It is the picture that must go with you into the grave, the picture of her who had the happiness of pleasing you enough so that you did not hesitate to offer to share your life with her, even when you had seen her only a few times. You often told me that this was the only occasion in your life when you acted without hesitation, with the absolute conviction that you were doing well. My Pierre, I think you were not wrong. We were made to live together. . . . Everything is over, Pierre is sleeping his last sleep beneath the earth; it is the end of everything, everything, everything."

Eighteen years earlier, Marie had written about never letting "one's self be beaten down by persons or events." Pierre's death certainly could have beaten her down. But Marie's strong sense of duty carried her through. But without Pierre, she was like he had described once, "like a body without a soul."

Pierre's income was gone now. Marie had to find some way to support her two daughters and father-in-law. The French government offered to give her a national pension. Marie refused, saying she was "young enough" to work.

The Sorbonne wanted to keep Marie on their staff,

Marie and her two daughters.

but they weren't sure how to do it. Who could they put in the laboratory in Pierre's place? Marie was a genius. Could she work *under* someone other than Pierre? And who could take Pierre's teaching job?

Jacques and a friend, Georges Gouy, went to the dean of the Sorbonne. They told him that Marie was the *only* French physicist capable of continuing Pierre's work. They insisted that she was the only teacher worthy of replacing him. She should not work under *anyone*.

The Sorbonne was in a troublesome position. No woman had ever been allowed to be a professor at the Sorbonne. But in May, the Sorbonne broke tradition and gave Pierre's job to Marie. They paid her 10,000 francs a year.

The children spent that summer with relatives. Marie studied Pierre's notes, and prepared to begin teaching his class in November. That autumn, she left her house in Paris and moved to Sceaux, where Pierre had lived and was buried.

One day, Pierre's father came to Marie. He said, "Pierre is no longer here, Marie. You have no reason to go on living with an old man. I can quite easily leave you, go to live alone, or with my elder son."

Now Marie truly loved the "old man." She couldn't bare to think of losing a faithful friend. He was a companion to her and to her children. Marie wondered if Dr. Curie wished to leave. "If you went away it would hurt me. But you should chose what you prefer," she said unselfishly.

His reply was, "What I prefer, Marie, is to stay with

you always." He really hadn't wanted to go. He loved Marie and his grandchildren, and wanted to be with them.

On November 5, 1906, Marie began teaching her first class. It was an occasion of great excitement. Marie was very famous now. Everyone wanted to hear the great scientist, who was the first woman to lecture at the Sorbonne. Not only students, but sightseers and newspaper reporters were in the audience. Even distinguished professors from other universities had come to learn from Marie!

Marie visited Pierre's grave before going to the university. She was always anxious whenever she had to appear in public. This occasion was no different. The brisk, thin woman entered the hall promptly at 1:30. She placed her notes on the desk in front of her. She acted as if there were only interested students in the room, not this odd mixture of gawkers and intellectuals. To anyone who knew her, her nervousness was obvious. She rubbed her fingertips constantly, and shuffled her papers too much. But her voice, even though it was hard to hear, did not waver.

As she began to speak, some of the students began to weep. They recognized that Marie had started the course exactly where her husband had ended it. Her first sentence had been Pierre's last sentence to his class: "When one considers the progress that has been made in physics in the past ten years . . ."

When she had finished her first lecture in Pierre's place, she left the room very quickly.

In 1908, she honored her beloved husband by publishing the *Works of Pierre Curie.*

A year later, Pierre's father was confined to bed for a whole year with lung congestion. Marie was by his bedside every free moment, but all her nursing was useless. The old man died on February 25, 1910.

For several years after Pierre's death, Marie threw herself into work to ease the pain. She accomplished a great deal. In 1909, she published a work of her own titled, *Treatise on Radioactivity.* She did a second check on the atomic weight of radium. She also did some very dangerous research.

So far, Marie had only been able to produce radium salts. With the help of a scientist named Andre Debierne, she was able to obtain pure radium metal. It was one of the most difficult operations known to science. It was so difficult, it was never done again during her life time.

First she had to separate out large amounts of radium chloride. Through a process using electric current, she added mercury to that. This mixture was then distilled. The tiny amount of shiny, white solid left over was the radium metal.

Scientists were debating over whether radium was a metallic element. Most of them thought it was not. Marie took on this experiment to settle the question, and proved radium *was* a metallic element.

Marie also found a way to measure radium by measuring the rays it gave off. She created a "service of measures." Now, radioactive products could be studied and given a certificate showing their radium content.

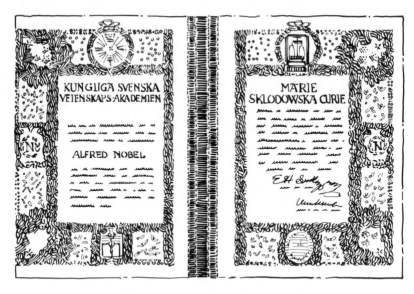

Nobel Prize.

In 1911, she prepared the first international standard for radium. It was 21 milligrams of chloride of pure radium, sealed in a light glass tube. The standard was deposited at the International Bureau of Weights and Measures. Throughout five continents, it served as a model for measuring radium.

In recognition of her work, Marie was given honorary degrees from universities all over the world. She never displayed any of them. She was so modest.

In December of 1911, Marie became the first person to receive a second Nobel Prize. This one was for chemistry, and it was to honor her for *all* her work on radium.

Although by now she was sick and weak with radiation poisoning, she went to Stockholm. Bronya and 14-year-old Irene went with her. At the ceremony, Irene watched her mother receive a prize that she herself would win many years later.

CHAPTER THIRTEEN

Dreams and War

A few months before Marie was awarded the Nobel Prize, scandal broke out. A Paris gossip magazine printed a shocking story about Marie. It claimed that Marie was responsible for breaking up the marriage of a fellow scientist. It was true that she and the man were good friends. But the magazine could not prove that Marie ruined his marriage. The scientist even prepared to fight a duel to defend Marie's honor. It was a pretty silly duel, though. The other dueler, who represented the scientist's wife, couldn't bring himself to shoot. He claimed he couldn't take away from France a great scientist. Since no one would shoot, eventually everybody went home.

In the middle of all this scandal and dueling, Marie was nominated to be a member of the French Academy of Sciences. At that time it was an all-male organization. There were many members who felt it should stay that way. This supposed scandal with a married man was all the Academy needed to keep Marie out.

This incident was very hard on Marie. She was able to travel to Stockholm to receive her Nobel Prize, but in late December, she collapsed. She was taken to a nursing home for treatment. There, the doctors found she had an infection of the ureter, which is a duct that leads from the kidneys to the bladder. She stayed in the nursing home until March. By then she was strong enough for an operation on her kidneys. After the surgery, she went to a house that Bronya had rented outside of Paris. She need rest and quiet.

In May, a delegation from Poland came to visit her there. They invited her to be the director of a new radium laboratory in Warsaw. It would have been a wonderful opportunity, as well as a chance to return to Poland. But Marie had had a dream close to her heart for six years now. It was to see a laboratory built in France that would be exactly what Pierre had always wanted. She knew she had to stay in Paris to accomplish that dream. So she sent two of her best assistants, who were both Poles, to take her place.

In June, she had a relapse of her kidney problems, and was taken to another sanatorium. After she gained strength, she moved to England to stay with a friend. The woman, Mrs. Ayrton, rented a house near Christchurch on the Hampshire coast. Marie's visit was kept a secret so that she could get some much needed rest. Clad in a dark cloak, Marie enjoyed walking along the cliffs near the house. When she was stronger, Irene and Eve visited her. Mrs. Ayrton entertained seven-year-old Eve by playing her nursery songs on the piano. She talked to Irene about mathematics, as if the serious teenaged girl were an adult. Marie remained in England until the beginning of October.

In 1913, Marie attended the dedication of the Warsaw

laboratory. She was greeted with admiration by the Poles, but ignored by the Russians. One of the ceremonies was held in the Museum of Industry and Agriculture. Twenty-two years earlier, Marie had done her first laboratory work there! For the first time in her life, Marie was able to give a scientific lecture in Polish. She was finally speaking to her people in her native tongue. And she was talking on the subject that was closest to her heart. It was a perfect day for Marie!

The next day a banquet was given in her honor. In attendance was a very old woman with white hair. It was Miss Sikorska, the director of the first school Marie had attended. The old woman gazed at her former student with deep pride. Marie saw her in the crowd. She rose from her seat, and walked through the tables. When she reached the old woman, she impulsively kissed her on both cheeks. This was the same gesture the girls received in school. They were always kissed when school prizes were given out. It was such a tribute from her little Manya, that Miss Sikorska burst into tears. The audience showed its appreciation for Marie's gesture by applauding wildly.

Marie visited all the places of her childhood and youth. She wrote that such visits were both sweet and sad. It was not easy to bid her country goodbye, even though France was now her home.

Several months later, Marie's health had improved greatly. She was so much better, she took her daughters on a vacation in the Alps. The group they traveled with included Albert Einstein. The two great scientists spent many contented hours talking about science while Marie's daughters and Einstein's son enjoyed the scenery.

In 1914, Marie saw her dream for Pierre's laboratory come true. The Pasteur Institute had opened in 1888. It was a leading center for teaching and research on contagious diseases. The Institute also provided a clinic for medical treatment. In 1911, Marie had been offered a position there. The Sorbonne had not wanted to lose her. So the Sorbonne and the Pasteur Institute came up with a plan. They hoped it would make Marie happy. They offered to build a two-building laboratory on a street named after Pierre Curie. One building would house a laboratory for radioactivity, with Marie as its director. The other building would be a laboratory for biological research and Curietherapy. A famous doctor, Professor Claude Regaud, would be in charge. Marie accepted.

She insisted that both buildings be built with large rooms and big windows. She wanted a building that would serve its purpose long after she was dead. She picked out the flowers, trees, and bushes that would surround the two buildings. She even planted some of them herself. She wanted to have as large a part as possible in the creation of this building.

In July of 1914, the Radium Institute of Paris on the Rue Pierre Curie was completed. Professor Regaud had moved in. Marie would move into her half of the Institute in the fall. Meanwhile, her children were on vacation in Brittany. She planned to join them in August.

That month a terrible event changed both her plans and those of the whole world. World War I had begun.

Einstein and Marie.

It was impossible for the girls to return to Paris now. Marie was terribly worried. She wrote to her children on August 2, "The Germans have entered France without a declaration of war. We shall not be able to communicate with each other easily for some time."

As the Germans drew closer to Paris, people began to flee the city. But Marie didn't want to leave. She wanted to serve her adopted country. But how? With what weapons? Then it came to her. Perhaps she could use her knowledge of X-rays to help the wounded. Doc-

The radium institute at Paris.

tors used X-ray machines to find bullet pieces, or schrapnel, in wounded soldiers. Hospitals on the front lines of battle didn't have enough X-ray equipment. Marie had never actually worked with X-rays, but she'd lectured about them. She came up with a plan to take the X-ray equipment as close to the troops as possible.

Marie took on a task that was not easy for this shy, withdrawn woman. She began to approach people to help her collect the equipment she needed. Money and equipment came from all kinds of places—from the Sorbonne, from rich people, and from X-ray machine manufacturers. Cars and trucks were donated to Marie's project. Soon she had 200 of what she called "radiological cars." They were used to transport X-ray machines to field hospitals. The cars came to be called "Little Curies." Marie also trained young women to use the X-ray machines. From 1916 to 1918, more than 150 women were trained to work in the front line hospitals.

A Renault car, which had a truck-like body, was made into a radiological car for Marie. Throughout the war, she visited the wounded in her own "Little Curie."

Before she began this work, Marie realized there was one more task she had to do. It was important enough to leave Paris for a short while.

In her Paris laboratory she had one precious gram of radium. She had set aside the gram as a gift to her lab. It was not to be owned by any one person. Marie couldn't bear the thought that this gram of radium might be destroyed. Even worse, it could fall into the wrong hands. She decided to take it where she thought it would be safer. Marie boarded a train for Bordeaux, a small city not far from Paris. The radium's lead-lined case was so heavy she could not lift it alone. She spent the night in a hotel in Bordeaux. The next morning, she deposited the case in a bank vault, then took the first train back to Paris. The train she'd taken out of Paris had been filled with fleeing citizens. The train she took back to the city was full of soldiers. It was evident that the war was getting closer.

Marie during World War I in x-ray transport car.

Despite that, Marie wanted her children with her in Paris. Eve enrolled in school. Irene was now 17, and a pretty young woman. She wore her dark hair swept back from her face. She had her mother's high, wide forehead, and grave expression. Irene also shared her mother's devotion to work. Marie took Irene with her in the Renault to visit the wounded. Marie taught Irene how to take X-rays. Irene learned quickly to use the equipment to find shrapnel. Eventually, Marie let Irene take her place in the front lines.

On July 28, 1916, Marie got a driver's license. She learned how to drive the Renault car herself and to do minor auto repairs. She wanted to be prepared, in case a call came in and her driver wasn't available.

Marie tried to see that as many hospitals as possible had X-ray equipment. Thanks to her efforts, 200 radiological rooms were created. Together, her radiological cars and hospital rooms helped more than a million injured men.

During the war years Irene and Eve hardly saw their mother unless she was sick in bed. Marie worked tirelessly to serve France. She travelled all over the country in her X-ray car. She helped in other ways, as well. Along with her second Nobel prize, she had been given a cash prize, as well. Until the war, she'd left the money in a Swedish bank. Now she took it out and bought some French War bonds with it. She never expected to be repaid, however. And she wasn't. Marie also tried to convince the bank officials to take the gold medals she'd received as scientific awards. When the bank officials refused, she thought they were very foolish. What did she need with medals, when France could use the gold to help with the war?

She had moved into her new laboratory on the Rue Pierre Curie. In 1915, she brought the gram of radium back from the bank vault in Bordeaux and put it to use. It had been learned that radon, the gas given off by radium, could be used to treat scar tissue. Marie assigned some of her lab assistants to draw off the radon. The gas was sealed in tiny glass tubes and sent to various hospitals.

It was becoming clearer and clearer that radium could be dangerous. Marie seemed strangely unwilling to recognize this fact. Exposure to radiation and the radon was making her assistants sick. They became so ill that they

Marie and x-ray machine.

had to go to the country to recuperate. They would re-cover in the fresh air and came back to work healthy. So Marie didn't take their illnesses seriously. She herself never rested. When there was no one left to draw off the radon from the radium, she did it. It seems she was not as effected by the radiation as the others were. When she was ill, she would try to ignore it and keep on working. During the war some fellow scientists came to visit her in her lab. They described her as "rather grey and worn and tired."

What she had to see during the war had also effected her greatly. She recorded in her notes that she could never forget the terrible destruction of human life and health. She had seen so many men and boys dying of their in-juries, and many others recovering slowly, with pain and suffering.

CHAPTER FOURTEEN

A Special Gift

In August, 1918, the war was over! And, what's more, Poland was soon to be free! Marie couldn't believe it! She wrote to her brother Joseph that, "We did not hope to live to this moment . . . and it is here!" Poland's freedom gave Marie great comfort, after the past few years of war and tragedy. The war ruined her physically, and interrupted her work. Her money was gone. To support herself and her children she had only her professor's salary. For two more years she continued to train people in radiology. She also wrote a book, *Radiology in War*. And, once again, she returned to running her lab.

Irene was now 21. She wanted to follow in her mother's footsteps and study radium as a physicist. Eve had turned to music. The two daughters were not alike at all. Irene was brusque, and kept to herself. Like her mother, her first love was science. Her dress was similar to Marie's—dark clothes for lab work. Eve was like a flower by contrast, loving gaily colored dresses and hats. Both girls were pretty, but Eve seemed prettier because she wore a happier expression. Marie loved them equally. In a letter on September, 1919, she told them they were her "great fortune."

After the war, Marie's life seemed to fall into order again. She worked hard, but she also allowed herself to take vacations. She loved Brittany, especially the village of Larcouest on the Channel coast. At first she rented a cottage, and later had one built there. The Curie family loved that area. The houses they lived in had wonderful views of the sea. Many of the professors from the university liked to visit there, too. A witty journalist had nicknamed the place, "Port Science."

Marie and her girls sailed, swam, and rested. When she was more than 50 years old, Marie taught herself to swim. Eve said she was one of the best swimmers of her generation.

In May of 1920, A New York City magazine editor, named Mrs. William Meloney, came to interview Marie in her laboratory. Mrs. Meloney asked Marie what she would most like to have. Marie told her that she needed radium to continue her research. She couldn't buy it because it was too expensive. At that time radium cost $100,000 for one gram!

Mrs. Meloney was surprised that Marie couldn't obtain radium. She wrote an angry article in her magazine. Marie, she said "had contributed to the progress of science and the relief of human suffering." Now, Mrs. Meloney went on, Marie was in the prime of her life. Yet, she was not being given the tools she needed. How would she be able to make any further contributions?

Mrs. Meloney, who's nickname was "Missy," had a mission. She would see to it that somehow, some way, Marie Curie got her radium.

Her plan was simple. She would launch a fundraising drive. She was sure American women would give money to buy Marie the radium. In less than a year, she was able to tell Marie the money was available. The radium could be hers! However, she asked one favor in return. Would Marie come to America for a visit, and accept the radium personally?

Marie was afraid of a country that clearly loved what she hated most—publicity. By now she was always tired, and her hearing and sight had begun to fail. But, for the radium, she would go to America with her daughters. Missy came to France to escort the Curies on board the ship *Olympic*. She arranged a tour of America that she thought wouldn't tire Marie out too much. Conferences, honorary degree ceremonies, and award-givings were arranged carefully. Irene now 23, and Eve, 16, enjoyed the trip. Marie found it exhausting right from the start. However, even as tired as she was, she never let the smallest thing go unnoticed. An amusing event occurred on board the ship.

In Paris, Marie had met a young American woman named Harriet Eager. She invited her along on the voyage. One day, on board, Harriet went to find Marie, who was late for lunch. She found the scientist standing in front of her opened closet door, looking upset. The problem? There was a light in the closet that wouldn't go out. Marie didn't want to leave the light on and waste electricity. The American girl assured her that when the door closed, a switch automatically turned off the light. Marie searched for the switch. None was found. She wasn't satisfied. The two stood puzzled in front of the closet for a while. Then Harriet came up with the perfect scientific solution. She invited the Nobel Prize winning scientist to stand *inside* the closet. That way Marie could see for herself that the light went out. Marie did so and Harriet closed the door. When Marie stepped out, she was delighted. "You are right, Harriet!" Arm in arm they went on to lunch.

The *Olympic* docked in New York. Immediately, Marie and her daughters began a hectic schedule. There were banquets, receptions, and trips to universities and factories. Marie's hand was shaken so enthusiastically, that she had to have it bandaged. She let her daughters endure the endless handshakes for her. May 19, 1921, was the day before she was to receive her radium from President Harding. The newspapers described her as looking, "shy, weary, and disinterested." She was exhausted, but not disinterested!

Even though she was so tired, she didn't forget for one second why she'd come to America. That night, she sat down with Missy and had an agreement drawn up. Ever since Pierre had died, some had questioned who should own the gram of radium she had produced. She didn't want the ownership of this new radium she was about to receive to be questioned. She had a formal document drawn up. It said that the radium was for her to use freely "in experimentation and in pursuit of knowledge." This made the radium the property of her laboratory.

On May 20, at four o'clock, Marie stood in the White

Marie Curie accepting gram of radium from President Harding.

House. She was dressed in a black lace dress. It was the same one she'd worn ten years earlier to accept her Nobel Prize. Even for this occasion, the frugal scientist had not bought anything new. She was given a mahogany covered, lead-lined, 110 pound case that was to house the radium. The actual radium was still at the factory. President Harding handed Marie a parchment and hung a key on a silken cord around her neck. It was the key to the case.

After the ceremony, Marie was not yet free to return to France. There were still places she was expected to visit.

Everywhere she went the press, admirers, and invited guests crushed in on her. She knew she needed radium, but the price she had to pay for it was dear. Three days after the ceremony at the White House, Marie collapsed. The tour of the western part of the United States had to be cancelled. Marie took only a quiet trip to the Grand Canyon with her daughters and a friend. She found even that a trial. Irene and Eve were entranced by the natural wonder of the canyon.

Eve later wrote a biography of Marie. In it she said this trip made her and Irene aware of how famous and admired their mother was.

On June 28, the Curies left to return to France, again on the *Olympic*. Marie was exhausted. Still, she was happy that she had "made a very small contribution to the friendship of America for France and Poland."

The radium, in its box, was locked in a safe. But to get it Marie had had to make great sacrifices. Years before, she and Pierre had agreed never to patent their method of getting radium. If they had a patent, Marie would have been rich enough by now to buy it. She would not have had to travel all the way to America to obtain it. Later, Marie wrote that a patent would have given them enough money to set up their own radium institute. They would not have had "the obstacles which were a handicap to both of us, and which are still a handicap for me."

Then she added, "Nevertheless, I am still convinced we were right." She admitted that the world needed practical people who got the most money for their work. But she said "humanity also needs dreamers." Dreamers were those who loved their work so much that they put all their time and energies toward it. They didn't have any time left to get the money to help them keep on working. She knew that she and Pierre were such dreamers. She also felt that she lived in a "well-organized society." There should be some way to help "dreamers," so they could work without worrying about money.

CHAPTER FIFTEEN

The Final Years

On May 15, 1922, the League of Nations made her a member of the International Committee on Intellectual Cooperation. Many other organizations had wanted her to join their causes. She had always refused. She didn't want to be involved with any group that was political. Working on the committee was different, though. She would work in Geneva, Switzerland, with brilliant people like Albert Einstein. She could also use her position as vice-president to work for science. One goal she had was quite different from one she and Pierre had had. She wanted scientists to be able to copyright their work. For example, a scientist might discover a method that a factory could use. The factory would have to pay the scientist for the right to use the method. The scientist could use the money to finance *more* scientific work. Her change of heart may have come from her own experience. She had to practically beg money from others to continue her research. Perhaps she didn't want future scientists to have to go through the same embarrassment.

On December 26, 1923, the Curie Foundation celebrated the twenty-fifth anniversary of the discovery of radium. Marie was honored on this occasion. Many important people gathered in an auditorium at the Sorbonne. Letters were read from many foreign universities, scientific societies, and various governments. Speeches were made. The French government gave Marie an annual pension of 40,000 francs.

During the next years, Marie returned to Poland four times. Now she was in a position to help her native land. Now that Poland was free, she wanted Warsaw to have a radium institute of its own. It would be a center for scientific research and treatment of cancer, like the one in Paris. The problem was that Poland was very poor after the war. Marie proposed a plan. The people of Poland would buy the bricks used to construct the building. She put Bronya in charge of the campaign. It was called "Buy a brick for the Marie SklodowskaCurie Institute!" There were also posters, stamps, and postcards advertising the plan. Slowly, brick by brick, the plan worked. In 1925, Marie went to Warsaw to see the cornerstone laid. It was a very happy moment for her. One of her dreams for Poland was finally coming true!

The building grew slowly, but surely, after that. Still there wasn't enough money to buy the radium needed for cancer treatment. Once again Missy came to the rescue. Mrs. Meloney and Marie had remained friends after Marie's 1921 visit to America. All Marie had to say was that she wanted the radium. Missy had another fundraiser, and the United States came up with the money for Marie. In October, 1929, Marie again went to America. This time it was President Hoover who gave her the money for Poland's gram of radium.

On this visit to America, Marie was invited to stay in the White House for a few days. This time her visit to the United States was much calmer. She'd written Missy, "I must not have in my program, autographs, portraits, and handshakes." Nor were there to be interviews, large banquets, or receptions. Reporters were to be kept as far away from her as possible. All she had to do on this trip was visit some laboratories. She did attend small receptions, along with scientific conferences. She also paid a visit to St. Lawrence University in Canton, New York. Today her likeness is sculpted on an entrance door there.

Marie seemed to enjoy this slower-paced visit. She wrote Irene about a ride from New York City to Long Island. A policeman on a motorcycle rode ahead of them, blaring his siren. Vehicles scattered off the road to let them by. "In this way we carried on like a fire-brigade off to a fire. It was all very amusing."

Just three days after Marie's "fire-brigade" ride, it was Black Thursday. That was the day of the stock market crash. The country had just collected funds to buy another country some radium. Now the United States was also in great money trouble. The Great Depression was about to begin as Marie headed home.

On May 29, 1932, Marie's dream of seeing a radium institute in Warsaw came true. She was there for the completed building's dedication. It would be her last trip to her homeland. In fact, she decided not to make any more international trips. After World War I, she had made a number of goodwill visits. She traveled to Brazil, Italy, Holland, Spain, England, Czechoslovakia, and Belgium.

She attended lectures, university ceremonies, and visited laboratories in those countries. She knew that just being there made the occasions special for others. She knew she shouldn't refuse to go, but she was still a private person. She wanted the same thing she'd always wanted, to work in her laboratory.

Unfortunately, in her last years, bad health kept her even from her work. She had known as early as 1920 that she was getting cataracts. That year she wrote Bronya, "My greatest troubles come from my eyes and ears." There was a constant buzzing in her ears that she said "persecuted" her. In this letter she admitted something for the first time. She said there might be a relationship between her work with radium and her bad health.

Her vision had become blurred. She tried to hide this from her laboratory assistants. She'd write notes to herself in large letters. Or she'd pretend to be able to see an assistant's experiments. The assistants were aware she didn't see well. But out of respect for this dedicated scientist, they never let on.

She had her first eye operation in 1923. Heavy bleeding followed the surgery, and Marie had to be nursed by Eve who was living with her. The bleeding was followed by double vision. Marie had to wear a pair of thick glasses until the double vision went away. While she was recovering from the operation, she was determined to keep on working. She asked her daughter Eve to help her write an article for the Encyclopedia Britannica. She wrote 30 more scientific papers between 1919 and 1934.

By 1930, Marie had had four eye operations. She

survived them and more, because she was determined to keep on working. A letter written to Bronya in September, 1927, said, "Sometimes my courage fails me and I think I ought to stop working and live in the country." But, she added, "I do not know if I could live without the laboratory."

Her life was her work, and her work was her life!

Her oldest daughter, Irene, had the same drive. Since the war she'd worked right beside her mother in the laboratory. She had also been working toward her own doctor's degree. In March, 1925, she was ready to do as her mother had done 12 years before. She turned in her thesis to the professors at the Sorbonne and went to answer their questions. Marie felt that if she went, she would attract too much attention. So she stayed away. Irene was as cool and poised as her mother had been. She discussed her research on the alpha rays of polonium. She, too, impressed the professors with her intelligence and reserve. She got her degree, and her mother was extremely proud.

In 1926, Irene became engaged to Frederic Joliot, one of Marie's laboratory assistants. After they were married, only Eve lived with her mother. The third floor apartment on the Ile Saint-Louis was still as bare as all of Marie's homes had been. There were huge windows which Marie didn't want curtained. She wanted to see the Seine, with its constant river traffic. On the floor was only one rug, a gift from a Romanian manufacturer. Hanging on the wall was one watercolor, which was also a gift. Eve thought she might like to be a musician, so Marie bought her a grand piano. How empty the apartment must have seemed!

Eve proved to be an animated companion for her mother. She made friends easily, and was often out in the evening on social occasions. Unlike her mother and sister, Eve dressed in the latest styles of clothing. Her mother didn't approve. Coming in to watch her prepare to go out, Marie would exclaim, "What dreadful heels! You'll never make me believe that women are made to walk on stilts. . . . And what sort of new style is this, to have the *back* of the dress cut out?"

Laughing tenderly, Eve would simply ignore her mother's objections. Off she'd go for a night on the town.

Marie built two houses, one at Larcouest and the other on the Mediterranean. She never cared for her homes as much as she cared about her laboratory. Even in her last years, she arrived at the lab at nine o'clock every morning. She would still try to work there until eight o'clock at night. Her chauffeur delivered her to the Radium Institute in the morning. There would always be students to greet her when she arrived. They wanted to ask questions, or to report on some experiment they were doing. Marie would give one student her complete attention. Then she would turn to the next and deal with his or her problem. Marie never resented the time students took from her own research. She felt it was important for her to teach these young scientists. After all, they were the future.

Early in 1932, Marie was walking to her lab when she fell and broke her wrist. This set off other health problems. The buzzing in her ears came back. The radiation burns on her fingertips began to get worse. In 1933, X-rays showed she had a gallstone. Rather than have an operation, she went on a special diet. It seemed to work. Within days she was back working in her lab.

Marie had good reason for not wanting to miss a day in the lab. Irene and Frederic were working on their atomic research, and Marie wanted to be near them. In January of 1934, the couple bombarded some aluminum with radiation. When they took the source of the radiation away from the aluminum, the aluminum itself gave off rays. They had discovered *artificial radioactivity*! This discovery was as important as the discovery of radium had been 40 years earlier. Now people could actually produce radioactivity and learn to use it. The next year, Irene and Frederic would win the Nobel Prize for this work.

At Easter in 1934, Bronya accompanied Marie to her house in the south of France. The trip was so exhausting that Marie fell into bed and wept in Bronya's arms. This was unlike Marie, but with Bronya she felt free to break down. However, the next morning she was more herself. By the time she returned to Paris, she was feeling better. She spent her good days at the lab and bad days at home. Even at home, she wouldn't stay in bed. She worked on a book!

For years Marie had had a fever that would come and go. It, too, was a sign of the radiation sickness. Every day now, it got worse and worse. Finally, the fever be-

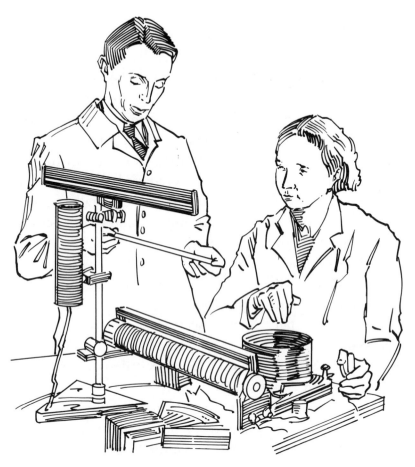

Irene Curie and husband.

came very high, then Marie would have violent chills. All the doctors could tell her was that she was over-worked! She didn't want to hear that. There was so much work she felt she had to do. She kept going to the lab until May of 1934. One afternoon she left work early, telling co-workers, "I have a fever, and I must go home."

113

After a brief visit to the gardens she had planted outside the institute, she left. She was never to return again.

Doctors were called to her home. They said she was having a return of tuberculosis. The treatment didn't help. As the days passed, she lay in bed growing weaker and weaker. Still she continued to think about the future. She made plans for the laboratory, for the institute in Warsaw, for her children. She predicted that Irene and Frederic would get the Nobel Prize. She even talked about a house that she had been wanting to build out in Sceaux where her husband was buried.

The doctors couldn't find out what was causing Marie's illness. Eve took her mother to a sanatorium in the mountains. She was called Mrs. Pierre so that no one would bother her. X-rays were taken again but they showed no tuberculosis at all! Her temperature was now up to 104 degrees! A blood test was ordered. It showed that her blood count was too low. Doctors now said she had severe anemia. Years later, doctors would know that Marie's anemia was caused by her work with radium. They would also know that radiation doesn't produce the same effects in everyone. Marie was obviously very strong. Others would not have lived as long as she did after working with radium.

She was now too ill to be moved from the sanitorium. To ease her pain, she was given medicine. Both Eve and the doctors refused to tell the scientific dreamer that she had an incurable disease. All she had were her dreams of the future, and no one was going to take them away.

Her temperature dropped steadily. Always the scientist, Marie took her own temperature every day, until she was too weak. Her mind began to draw away from the real world, and sink into the world inside her. Stirring a cup of yogurt, Marie asked, "Has it been made with radium or mesothorium?"

Her last words were to a doctor who came to give her a shot to kill her pain. "I don't want it," she said. "I want to be left alone." That is what she'd wanted all her life.

At dawn on July 4, 1934, Marie Sklodowska Curie, at age 66, finally died. Her death was caused by 30 years of exposure to her great scientific discovery—radium and its dangerous radioactivity.

She was buried right above Pierre in the family plot in Sceaux. Bronya and Joseph each threw earth from Poland into their little sister's grave. One year later, Marie's last book was published. She had finished writing it just before going to the sanatorium. It was titled *Radioactivity*, by Mrs. Pierre Curie, Professor at the Sorbonne, Nobel Prize in Physics, Nobel Prize in Chemistry. This was her last triumph. Marie Curie had given her health and her life to scientific works that benefited humankind. For Marie Sklodowska Curie, the words she'd written when she was 26 had proven true: "We must believe that we are gifted for something, and that this thing, at *whatever cost*, must be attained."

1. Why are X-rays so helpful to doctors?
2. What is an experiment?
3. How did Marie Curie finally help her beloved homeland of Poland?
4. Why was Marie Curie not elected to the French Academy of Arts and Sciences?
5. Why did the American journalist, Mrs. William Meloney, help Marie Curie? How did she do it?
6. Why did Marie Curie hesitate before agreeing to marry Pierre Curie? What convinced her to marry him?
7. When Marie was a young student in Poland, she had to study Polish history secretly. The Russians, who ruled Poland at the time, had made it illegal for schools to teach Polish history. Why do you think the Russians did this? Why did Marie and other Poles disobey this law?
8. When the Curies discovered how to separate radium from pitchblende they could have patented their discovery and made a great deal of money from it. Why didn't they?
9. Why do you think it took so long for Marie to admit that the radiation she was exposing herself to was dangerous?
10. When the Curies were doing their early experiments,

they worked long hours, under awful conditions, in drafty, leaky laboratories. Yet Marie later said it was the happiest time of their life together. Why do you think the Curies felt happy?

11. Pierre Curie believed that working for political change was not as important as working to make new scientific discoveries. He said to Marie that science could only benefit mankind. Do you agree or disagree with Pierre Curie? Why?

12. What gave Marie Curie the idea that there must be radioactive elements in addition to radium that had not been discovered yet?

Bolton, Sarah K. *Famous Men of Science*. Crowell, 1960 (Biographical sketches of famous scientists).

Curie, Eve (translated by Vincent Sheean). *A Biography of Marie Sklodowska Curie*. Doubleday, 1949 (Insightful, well-judged account by the daughter of the great woman).

Fermi, Laura. *The Story of Atomic Energy*. Random House, 1961 (A dramatic account from the ancient Greeks to the present day).

McKown, Robin. *She Lived For Science: Irene Joliot-Curie*. Messner, 1961 (A biography of the daughter of Marie and Pierre Curie, who, with her husband, Frederic Joliot, won a Nobel Prize of her own).

Riedman, Sarah. *Men and Women Behind The Atom*. Abelard-Schuman, 1958 (The story of atomic energy told through short biographical sketches).

Stepp, Ann. *The Story of Radioactivity*. Harvey House, 1971 (Well-written, comprehensive account of atomic structure and the effects of radiation).

artificial radioactivity
when certain substances which are not naturally radioactive are exposed to enough radiation, they will become radioactive themselves.

atoms
the smallest particle of an element. Scientists used to
believe that the entire universe was made up of these
tiny particles, and that no smaller particle was possible.
Now we know that atoms are made up of many even
smaller particles.

cataracts
a clouding of the lens of the eye which causes poor
vision and sometimes blindness.

Csar
(also spelled Tsar) the title of the rulers of Russia until
the Russian Revolution in 1917. The Csar who ruled
when Marie was a child was called Csar Alexander II.

Einstein, Albert
a very famous physicist who did much work in the area
of nuclear physics and who benefitted from the work
of Marie Curie.

ion
an atom that carries a positive or negative electric
charge.

laboratory
a place equipped to conduct experiments and scientific
research.

Latin Quarter
a section of Paris, France where the Sorbonne Uni-

versity and other schools are located. Many students, teachers, writers, and artists live there, which makes it a very lively neighborhood.

League of Nations

after World War I, many nations came together and formed this organization to work for world peace. This group did not last, but today its goals are carried out by the United Nations.

Manya, Manyusya

these are Polish nicknames for the name Marya, which is Mary in English and Marie in French.

molecule

a specific combination of atoms which create a substance with specific properties. For example, two atoms of the element hydrogen and one atom of the element oxygen join together in a specific way and form a molecule of the substance, water.

Nobel Prize

every year in Stockholm, Sweden, a panel of judges award this prize to the people who have benefitted humanity in the greatest way in various areas, including science, literature, medicine, and peace. Marie Curie won two Nobel Prizes in science.

nuclear

relating to the central part of the atom, called the nucleus, and also relating to the energy which comes from atoms.

Periodic Table

a chart which arranges all the elements according to their atomic weight, and which shows other important relationships between them.

pernicious anemia

a serious disease marked by a decrease in the number of red blood cells. The symptoms include paleness, weakness, stomach and intestinal disorders, and nervous disturbances.

physics

a branch of science that deals with matter and energy and their interactions. Within this branch of science are included the fields of mechanics, acoustics, optics, heat, electricity, magnetism, radiation, atomic structure, and nuclear phenomena.

pitchblende

a shiny brownish–black mineral that contains uranium and radium.

polonium

a radioactive element that is found in pitchblende, discovered by Marie Curie who named it after her native country, Poland.

radiation

energy which is emitted in the form of waves or particles. This general definition includes all forms of radiated energy including light and heat. (This word is often used specifically to mean the harmful radiated energy which is emitted by radioactive substances.)

radiation sickness

sickness that results from exposure to radiation. Symptoms include weakness, vomiting, loss of hair and teeth, burns on the skin, bleeding, loss of red blood cells, and death.

radioactivity

the property possessed by certain elements, such as uranium and radium, of spontaneously emitting radiated energy.

radium

an intensely radioactive metallic element that is found in minute quantities in pitchblende. It was first discovered and isolated by Marie Curie.

Sorbonne

a famous university in Paris.

tuberculosis

a serious and very contagious disease of the lungs marked by much weakness and coughing. In previous centuries the disease killed many people, but today it is rare.

treatise

a careful and systematic report giving the facts of the case, explaining the principles involved, and stating what conclustions were reached.

typhus

a severe disease marked by high fever, intense headache, a red rash, and mental disturbances.

uranium

a silvery radioactive element that is found in pitchblende.

X-ray

a kind of radiation, one of whose properties is that it can pass through solid objects and make photographic images on film. This makes it very useful in medicine, to help "see" inside the body without surgery.